Mercedes Light and Dark

Mercedes Light and Dark

Michael Ugarte

Compass Flower Press
Columbia, Missouri

© 2022 Michael Ugarte

All rights reserved. No part of this book may be reproduced or transmitted in any form or by any means without permission from the author or publisher.

Published by Compass Flower Press
Columbia, Missouri

Library of Congress Control Number: 2022902995
ISBN: 978-1-951960-32-2 Trade Paperback
ISBN: 978-1-951960-34-6 Ebook

To the memory of my brother George Ugarte Precioso (1943-2017) who would have had lots to say about this memoir had he lived to read it.

The act of considering my mother's life is an act of love.

—Richard Ford

*Now as I write my life in 1835, I make many discoveries . . .
I discover the shape and the "why" of past events.*

—Stendhal

TABLE OF CONTENTS

Acknowledgements xi
Prologue xv

Part I
1. For the Record—Mercedes' Mental Malady 3
2. Somewhere between New Hampshire and Vermont 15

Part II
3. Going Back to a Time You Cannot Know 25
4. Mercedes in the Revolution 45
5. Mercedes after the Revolution 63

Part III
6. Setting Sail for Life in New England 81
7. Mercedes' Mental Malady Revisited 89
8. Faculty Wife 99
9. Leaping into the Gorge 115

Part IV
10. One Hundred Years of Solitude 141
11. Golden (Not-So-Golden) Years in Missouri 157
12. The South Hampton Death House 171
Epilogue: A Speck in the Horizon 183
Family Tree 195
Related Reading 197

Acknowledgments

I want these modest remembrances of my mother to be a gift to my family, especially my two children, in the hopes that this work might encourage them to ponder those old questions: Who am I and where did I come from? And the same goes for non-family members, anyone who reads this book.

There are many people who have had a hand in guiding me along the path of recreating my mother's life. I'm certain some of Mercedes' friends and family do not remember her in the same way that I do, but I hope those people forgive me for my faulty memory. That forgiveness (or non-forgiveness) does not detract from my gratitude.

Thank-you to my son Francisco (Cisco) and my daughter Maura (Molly). Maura's photos of her grandmother are an important part of this memoir. The photo that graces the cover of this book is hers. To Hillary and her mom and dad, Amir and Lani. To Ryan (Raúl) who had some raucous laughs with Grandma. To Kathleen who laughed occasionally with Mercedes. To Maurita who laughed too and put up with a lot of grief. And to her family, the Pleasant Street McCarthy's. A special remembrance of her brother Paul (RIP).

A huge debt of thanks to my loving partner María (Marí) Mercedes (the name is just a coincidence) who was born and raised in the same area of Spain as my mom (again just a coincidence). To her daughter Mar for her insights about the Spain of my mom's generation also to Mar's husband Nav. To Marí's son Francisco José and his partner Ana. To all my grandchildren, Maelle, Frankie, and Alma on my side; Sofía and Alba on Marí's side.

To my brother's family, Rosi, Patti, Mercedes, Christopher, Becky, Cita, and especially to George Andrew Ugarte, my brother's first born, who was close to his grandma Mercedes. Thanks to Andy for all the visits to Hanover when he was a student at Boston College; my mom had fond memories of Andy. Thanks also to Andy's mother, Margie.

To my mother's family in Spain, her sister, my Tía Marina (RIP) whose energy, elegance, and thoughtfulness I will never forget; I think of her every day.

My aunt Sole too (RIP), so kind to me when we went back to Hellín and to her husband Juan. To all my cousins and their spouses, Maruja, Amado, Marina, Mercedes, Juanjo, Javier and Belén. Posthumous thanks to César (RIP), Madalen (RIP) and Juan Luis (RIP).

There are two relatives whom I especially want to acknowledge for giving me specific information about the family: Amado Precioso Giménez and Javier López Precioso. Amado in particular related his memories of the family in Hellín. Another family member who helped me is Luis Nogueras Estradé, mi cousin Marina's husband (on my dad's side) who has compiled a genealogical list of the Ugartes from Orozco, 1561 to the present, "Genealogía De Ugarte."

Thanks also to Mercedes' brother Artemio (RIP), my Tío Artemio who was a prominent environmental activist in the last stage of his life, one of the founding members of Greenpeace in Spain. Thanks also to Artemio's daughter Amaya and her husband Mario for their encouragement.

There are lots of non-family members I want to thank: Justin Butler who read a short part of the manuscript and who recited a poem at a gathering at the now defunct Cherry Street Artisan, as well as to the entire poetry class in the Department of Romance Languages at MU (circa 2004) who recited verses at that café. To all those who attended my mom's two funerals: one in Columbia, the other in Hanover, NH where she is buried alongside of Paco. To Joe Polacco who knows what it's like to write about one's mother. To my best friend Dennis who remembers my mom with fondness, regardless (or because of) all her eccentricities.

My friend, Prof. Francisco Linares, who has taken on the task of investigating my grandfather's life, has been an invaluable help to me: thanks to Paco for the many emails and prompt replies to my queries. On that same note, my friend for almost a decade, Prof. Gonzalo Álvarez Chillida of the History Department at the Universidad Complutense of Madrid showed me how to navigate the libraries and archival collections in Madrid and its environs. I asked him lots of specific questions about the Civil War and he replied to me immediately.

To Dr. Miguel Marín Padilla (Dartmouth Medical School) who was, with his wife Tere, my mom and dad's good friend. Thanks also to my mother and father's life-long friends Bob and June Russell (both RIP). To Prof. Maite Núñez Betelu who wrote a wonderful piece about my father in a collection of essays on Basque exiles of the Spanish Civil War.

To the institutions and libraries that I consulted: Centro Documental de la Memoria Histórica in Salamanca, Archivo Histórico Provincial de Cádiz, Instituto de Estudios Albacetenses, especially Antonio Silva. Also, to University of Missouri Peace Studies Program.

Mavi Fuentes and Armando León-Sotelo both knew Mercedes well. When I told them that I was writing a memoir about her, they encouraged me. So much so that I asked Mavi, an accomplished translator, to translate this work into Spanish. A mutual friend, Rafael Reig, also encouraged me to write non-academic things; I'm grateful for the encouragement.

I've saved the editors for last because I want to give them a very special note of appreciation. To Yolanda Ciolli not only for her enthusiasm about this project but especially her sensitive eye regarding format and photography. Evelyn Rogers of the *Missouri Review* was one of the first readers. Her kind words and excellent suggestions *gave* me a big boost. And to Theresa Cameron for a thorough reading and some excellent suggestions.

Prologue

I am the son of Spanish immigrants to the United States who ventured off from their country after a grueling civil war, a departure that landed them in the peaceful confines of Hanover, New Hampshire, where I grew up. I like to think of them as "emixiles," or emigrant-exiles, because they were fleeing from the shackles that a bloodthirsty general (whose name was Franco) had created in their country, while they were also seeking well-being elsewhere, like anyone simply looking for a better place to live.

But I often ask myself why I use the plural *they* when I speak of my parents' experiences and motivations. To assume that these two people formed part of a unified whole, as in "my better half," or in Spanish, *mi media naranja* (my half orange), or that they saw the same things, or felt the same emotions, isn't the whole picture, not even half of it. My father was a professor at Dartmouth College for twenty-three years; he often told his life story to his students, to his children, his friends, his family back in Spain, and at times to total strangers. He wrote some of it down; as a professor he was obligated to write, and narrating his experiences was a way to fulfill that obligation, an obligation he accepted with pleasure, at times with glee. Given the sensibilities of his times (1910-1969), it's not the least bit surprising that he (and everyone around him, including his children) thought his experiences were integrally connected to those of his life companion.

It's not that he was wrong—he couldn't tell the story of his life without at least a mention of his wife; but he wasn't right either. His wife Mercedes lived her own life about half with him and half without him. Her mother died when she was a child, her father suffered persecution both before and after the Spanish Civil War, she accompanied her husband on his bold departure from Spain to the United States after the war. She was the loving wife of a man who was at that time a diplomat, and he was also her uncle. Yes, that's one of the major perplexities of this book. Some might call it incest or inbreeding, but that's not right. I'll call it what some of my family members called it: *una relación sanguínea* (a blood relation), perhaps not so uncommon years ago. In any case, I'll get into that in these pages. In the new country where her husband managed to land a job teaching at Dartmouth College, she became the proverbial "faculty wife" until he died a tragic death, after a long bout of bi-polar disturbance. After his death she spent three decades living alone sorrowfully and joyfully in Hanover, New Hampshire, with occasional visits from her two boys, George and Michael. She too suffered several periods of mental illness, one of which landed her in a "retreat" in Vermont in the 1950s. She also suffered reduced capacity by dementia in her final years, a mental deterioration I witnessed every day after she moved to Columbia, Missouri, to be with me, her second-born son, then in my fifties.

Most who knew her thought she was charming, unique, quick to smile, prone to fantasy and exaggeration, and very Spanish, as her U.S. friends used to say, especially in light of a heavy accent that she never got rid of. However, she was not always charming; she could be outright mean, judgmental, demanding, haughty, paranoid, narcissistic, shrill, and utterly annoying. Those other moments, often unpleasant or infuriating to me, remain perplexing. *Crazy*. I'm not sure there's a better word in all its acceptations—extreme, dramatic, unstable, wild, absurd, abnormal, and yes, even fun, as in "a wild and crazy gal." I didn't understand then, and don't fully understand now, where all her flights of fancy were coming from.

And that's what this book is about—it's about the other half. My dad had his own sadness, contradictions and mental affliction. He was equally complicated, and these pages will attest to that. But he has been the object of much of the outside attention, while my mom seemed to fall by the wayside without much scrutiny. While my memory of my dad is at once tender and disturbing, as fraught as it is, my mom was another entity entirely, and I hold another set of memories. While she was a dedicated wife and mother, she wasn't half of anything—perhaps a greater enigma than my father even today, thirteen years after her death.

To this day, after all those years with her, against her, away from her, close to her, encircled by her, and entrapped by her, I remain perplexed. It's not just curiosity, or a difficult query I'm determined to solve, or an obsession. It's all those things and more. Mercedes has to do with who I am—my core, my past, my children, my present and future. As I try to figure out my mom, I try to figure out myself. She gave me life in many more ways than one; there is nothing I do or feel today that does not reveal or disguise the trace of Mercedes in some way. And I wager I'm not the only one with a mother they're still trying to figure out. I'm convinced that even those fortunate enough to have come to terms with their mothers, when they search a little behind the surface or concentrate on that quirky incident that happened years ago, they just might succumb to the same sense of wonderment I feel when I think about my mom.

Yes, a sense of wonderment. Listen to what Zora Neale Hurston says in *Their Eyes Were Watching God* about how women make use of Memory (although she doesn't capitalize it—that's me): "Now, women forget all those things they don't want to remember, and remember everything they don't want to forget. The dream is the truth. Then they act and do things accordingly."

That's my mother, and that's what made writing her Memory at once frustrating and exhilarating. Countless times, when I asked my mom to try to remember something, she looked at me with a glazed expression as if to say, "Never mind."

To this day, after many years of trying to understand my mom with the help of those who knew her—especially my son, Francisco, and daughter, Maura—after all that pondering and discussion, with many books, documents, and photos at my disposal—I still have no clear idea. But I have lots of hazy notions, sensations, theories, imaginings, and most important, memories. I say most important because I feel Memory has taken on a special role: it's become an aid as well as an obstacle, a friend and an enemy, something real and a fantasy, a fact that becomes a fiction the more I ponder it. My struggle (this book)—at once fulfilling and excruciating—to remember my mom's life, even the parts that took place before I was born, is a sporadic one. It's filled with interruptions and musings. Don't look for a neat chronological narrative—to put my mother in that kind of box is contrary to her own life and persona. I want to be true to that persona (in both the English and Spanish sense of that word).

In the final analysis, it is my deepest hope that my recollections might have something everybody can recognize, even though at times I just can't be sure of their accuracy. But then again accuracy, I have come to understand, is secondary to the emotional truth that memories convey.

Mercedes remains on my mind, crying out to me as if to say, "Getting over me, Miguel, is impossible, and understanding me is just as hard, but I dare you to try."

So, reader, come along and take the ride with me.

Part I

Chapter One

For the Record—Mercedes' Mental Malady

I have a nagging urge to find out more about my mother than what I remember. But what happens when facts interfere with Memory? For me, that persistent itch was a discomfort that started the very day my mom told me she had spent time in a mental hospital. So I decided to do something about that itch and try to find out if my mom was really crazy.

A few years ago, I wrote a letter to the directors of the still-operating Brattleboro Retreat in Vermont, requesting information about Mercedes Ugarte, on the slim chance there would be a record of her.

To my amazement, I received a thirty-six-page detailed report of her stay. This was her "anamnesis" as they titled it, a medical history containing conversations with several psychiatrists, diagnoses, results of physical examinations, my father's letter describing the situation to the administrator of the facility, doctors' interviews with my mother, descriptions of her encounters with nurses, and some, not many, numbers. They sent me what purported to be a scientific narrative of her psychotic episodes, although much of it (the most interesting part) was based on speculation—professional opinions on what was troubling her and why.

What I found surprising was that the report contained not the assessment of just one psychiatrist, but several, all interested in her illness and well-being. From what I surmise, the doctors must have had a conference to decide if she was well enough for the hospital to discharge her under the supervision of my father. As the wife of a professor at Dartmouth, she was well attended.

Here are the facts as recorded in the Case of Mercedes P. Ugarte (the husband's surname), anamnesis number 14619:

Name—Mercedes P. Ugarte; Age—35; Admitted—Feb. 23, 1949; Residence—Hanover, NH; Nativity—Spain; Occupation—Housewife; Religion—Catholic; Maintenance—Private; No. of Attack—First; Duration—About a week; Diagnosis—Manic-Depressive Psychosis; Previous Admissions—None; Correspondent—Francisco Ugarte (husband), 9 South Park St. Hanover, NH; Discharged—March 13, 1949; To—Husband; Result—Recovered. [Recovered? Not really. These episodes would recur but with less severity. I say that after reading the anamnesis, but as I try to recall the instances when my mom went bonkers, I'm sure those later bouts of "manic-depressive psychosis" (today bipolar) came back to haunt her, and today they are haunting me.]

Complaint—During the birth of her son [Michael], *the patient resented and resisted the gas used during the delivery. She was becoming psychotic; she had fears related to her suspicion that her family was being investigated for being communists. She was hearing noises, which she was apt to misinterpret.*

Family Background—Her father, Artemio Precioso, was a financially successful novelist and journalist. With the turn of events in Spain he lost his fortune and moved to Paris. When the Republic was declared in Spain he returned to form part of the government. He was appointed Governor of the province of Toledo. When civil war broke out he was persecuted by anarchists and communists. In 1936 he was condemned to death. The sentence was commuted to four years. After his release, he was a broken man. [Indeed "a broken man." Mercedes would agree, but the sentence was commuted to eight years, not four; he spent the last two years of his life under house arrest.]

The patient's mother, Marina Ugarte, was born in Brussels. She was the sister of the patient's husband. [True, as strange as it sounds.] *At age twenty-six she died in the flu epidemic of 1918. The father remarried. Artemio had three children with the first wife: Mercedes, the oldest, followed by Marina, and Artemio. With the second wife the father had three daughters. The eldest daughter of that group is quite stupid and poor.*

The patient and her husband are close to the children of the first marriage. Marina is married to Amado Giménez. They both live in Hellín and are doing well. Amado has played along with Franco, decidedly conservative in politics.

Artemio [my mom's brother, named after his father] *joined the Communist Party in 1936 when he was seventeen. He fought with the Loyalist [anti-Franco] troops, and at the end of the war escaped by plane from the grasp of Franco. The family received news through a postcard sent from Oran, Africa. The family heard nothing from him until 1946 when they received a card informing them he was in Moscow. He was married, settled, and remained a communist.*

The father of the husband, who was also the grandfather of the patient [that sounds weird, but he was; my father married his niece], *was somewhat mentally ill toward the end of his life. He was a mining engineer. He always had visionary schemes to make a large amount of money. He was irresponsible; sometimes he ran in the streets improperly clad. He fought with the servants. At one time his relatives placed him in an asylum, but he stayed there for a short time. The patient and her husband have not heard from him in two years. He is eighty-four and apparently living in the Canary Islands. The pretty definitely authentic tradition of the family is that said grandfather had two sisters who were demented.* [Now there's a discovery. I don't remember my mother or my father telling me that Javier Ugarte Schultz, my paternal grandfather, had two "demented" sisters. I later learned that he died the year I was born.]

Personal History—When the patient was five years of age, her mother died. She suffered from the temperament and disposition of her father; she was distressed by the loss of the family fortune and by her father's imprisonment which followed. While she was well protected during the war by virtue of her husband's position, there was always anxiety about the rest of the family. She applied for citizenship after coming to this country.

Education—Her education was rather unofficial, partly in private schools, tutors, and secondary schools. At one time she went to an elementary junior college. She has not been deeply devoted to her studies. It was the tradition in the family that a daughter should marry and settle in homes of their own.

Occupational History—The patient has never been gainfully employed. [Woman's work: never called "gainful employment." Typical attitudes of the fifties, no matter if you're in the U.S. or in the Old World.] *She lives with her husband in Hanover and occasionally assists him in Spanish conversation classes.*

Menstrual History—The menstrual function of the patient is regular.

Marital History—Patient was married to Francisco Ugarte, now thirty-nine years of age, September 27, 1935. Before the marriage he studied business administration at Rutgers University at his own expense. He returned to Spain to study law at the University of Madrid. He achieved a law degree equivalent to an American PhD. [Not sure what they mean by that.] *He became an official translator at the American Embassy in Madrid. At the outbreak of the war he was left in charge of the Embassy, as he gave protection to 150 Americans who had taken refuge in the Embassy. He received a letter of commendation signed by Cordell Hull. In May of 1946 he entered the United States with his wife. They lived in Washington, DC, for two months. They then went to Hanover, where the informant was an instructor in Spanish.*

After the marriage, the patient lived with her husband in the American Embassy. During the years of the civil war her father was imprisoned for his alleged political crimes. The patient and her husband lived the kind of happiness which seemed to be dependent on each other and not upon any external situation. She was devoted to her family. She said her life was 90 percent her family. After moving to the United States, she was stressed because of the strange situation, and she was rather homesick. She did not make friends and was not becoming accustomed to American ways. Sexually their adjustment has been satisfactory. She responds adequately, not interested in matters of sex as some might be. They live in a four-room apartment owned by the college.

They have two children, George, five and a half, and Michael, just born. George's birth was a grueling sixteen-hour experience. The mother did not have the comfort of any sedative medication. Despite this, the child grew well, a fine healthy boy now quite popular with the children in Hanover. The patient was happy with her second pregnancy, not terrified at the thought of having a second child. The birth was quite natural; she was only in the hospital for an hour and a half before the baby was born.

Medical History—The tonsils of the patient were removed in 1931. In 1947 she had an attack of gallstones.

Personality—The patient has been a family woman. She had a deep love for her husband as well as undying loyalty toward all the members of her family. She has been deeply interested in her brother who has become a communist and in the brother-in-law who has been loyal to Franco. She is moody and exceptionally sensitive. There is a tendency to be suspicious of people's motives. She has called her husband "a candid fool and credulous" because she believes he accepts everything at face value. She enjoys going to movies at times with faculty wives. As a housekeeper she is immaculate; perhaps excessively so. She is not a member of any organizations. She goes to the Roman Catholic Church with her husband, but they have not gone to confession for many years. [Yes, if my mother ever went to confession when she lived in New Hampshire, her intentions were not always honorable: she went to flirt with the priests.]

Present Illness—According to the informant, the patient's illness cannot be understood apart from the stress caused by the faculty circle in the Department of Romance Languages at Dartmouth. The patient's and informant's first friend in Hanover was Professor Pianca, who taught Spanish and Italian. He is a graduate of Dartmouth and has been a professor there for many years. There was also a Professor Arce from Costa Rica. Prof. Pianca told the informant that as long as he had someone to push him along, he would be promoted. The informant reacted to this negatively, as he believed that his promotion should be based upon merit. There was a meeting in which Professors Pianca and Arce argued that not only should the informant be denied promotion, but that he should be dismissed. But another friend of the informant arose to his defense and convinced the majority of the department to promote, a painful victory for the informant. At that time, the informant and the patient discussed the situation at length. Both were puzzled by the turn-around of those who purported to be their friends; they suffered as a result. While the patient was worried about what the neighbors would think, for the informant the case was resolved. There was no unusual distress until the birth of the second child. On the second day after the birth, Dr. Boardman, the pediatrician, felt that the patient was developing a psychosis. The informant at first resisted this opinion, but later noted that his wife was developing ideas of persecution. She became convinced that she and her husband were being investigated for being communists and that the nurses and doctors were detectives. She had visions; she spoke incoherently. She spoke a great deal about the gas which was used as an anesthetic during the birth; she felt she could smell the gas for days after the birth. There was a boy crying in the hospital; she felt that it was her son George. Noises in the street disturbed her. She misinterpreted those noises and misinterpreted events in her past. She was a voluntary patient at the Brattleboro Retreat.

General Type, Appearance—Patient is well developed, well nourished, olive complexioned. Dark brown hair and brown eyes. Hair of female type of distribution. Nipples are pigmented dark brown. Blood pressure 134/90. Height 5' 1". Weight 142 pounds.

Admission Note (Feb. 23, 1949)—Patient was brought to Retreat by auto by her husband, accompanied by some friends—Mr. and Mrs. Denoeu and Mrs. Marshall, all in the French Department. According to Dr. McKenna at Mary Hitchcock in Hanover patient began to show mental symptoms. She had become increasingly confused, was sleeping poorly, did not cooperate, was becoming too much of a problem for the hospital to handle. Patient came into the general office with a smile, looked all around before sitting down. When questioned about her sickness, she spoke about her baby, then said she noticed noises all over the place. She spoke of having dreams and strange ideas. When told she was going to her new quarters, she looked around puzzled, and asked three or four times, "Where am I going?" She went along with her husband. She was assigned a bed in the North Dormitory.

Feb. 25—Patient was very excited, disturbed, and aggressive. She kept everyone on the ward awake, and when the nurses attempted to settle her, she would strike at them and scratch them. In the morning she was less disturbed, but this quietness did not last; it was soon reported that she was again excited, aggressive, and disturbing the other patients. It seemed advisable to transfer her to the east side where she can have [ice] packs and so that the other patients would have rest and not be disturbed by this patient's activities. The balance of her talk and excitement was that she must get back to her husband and her child and she not infrequently tried to get out of the door in order to get away to her husband and child.

Patient's Own Complaint (March 2)—"I want to be restful, treated well, and have a nice rest which I didn't in the hospital. In the Mary Hitchcock I was hearing too much noises. Voices talking and they make me talk and they make me very nervous and I couldn't sleep and everything in the hospital."

Attitude and General Behavior—Patient continues active and noisy. She was resistive to care; on repeated occasions assaulted the nurses while they were trying to give her the necessary attention. On one occasion she tore the uniform of Miss Horner and on another she pushed Mrs. Bonnett down while the latter was trying to put her in pack. Patient has required packs twice daily until today. This morning she appeared clearer mentally. When asked to come to the examiner for an interview, she was suspicious and asked whether other patients have to go through this routine. In the office, however, she relaxed.

Stream of Mental Activity, Content of Thought (March 2, 1949)—Patient speaks in broken English with a pronounced Spanish accent. [Broken English?

I wonder what fixed English is.] *Transcript of interview with patient is as follows:*

Q: *Why did your husband bring you here?*
A: *To take a rest.*
Q: *Have you been sick for a time?*
A: *Yes, the trouble was hearing too much noises.*
Q: *Who were the voices you heard?*
A: *Well, that what I don't know the voices were. I had a baby, I was going to have a baby so Doctor Boardman took me to have a baby.*
Q: *How soon after you had the baby did you feel so bad?*
A: *Very soon, was almost the next day I wasn't feeling so well. I have feeling at hospital like if they want to give me another operation but then make me sick. If I needed another operation why they don't tell me?*
Q: *Did you think people were investigating you?*
A: *Oh, my trouble was that if they were making an investigation of something either if you were communists or could be fascists, fascists we very sure weren't.* [You got that right, Mom.]
Q: *Did you believe that the others were against you thinking you were communist?*
A: *Well you know now in the United States, you have a very natural thing that because they were making investigation to everybody who is communist because he is against country. So it was natural that investigate us. I have a brother who is a communist, I mean during the war he was and now he has been in Russia and after that in Czechoslovakia and we receive letter back and forth.*
Q: *Do you think you were suspected of that?*
A: *Yes, that's right.*
Q: *Did you feel the nurses and doctors were detectives in the hospital?*
A: *No, maybe the doctors and nurses were forced by the person from the American government to watch us foreigners.*
Q: *Do you still believe so?*
A: *Maybe I was wrong.*
Q: *Did we spy on you in this building?*
A: *No.*
Q: *In the other building?*

A: Oh, that was awful there. I couldn't breathe. It always smelling dust and I feel very bad like become crazy. The people in Tyler aren't normal.

Q: Did the gas at the hospital make you feel bad?

A: Yes, it makes me kind of nervous, no breathe.

Q: Do you still hear your baby crying at the hospital?

A: I was always hearing the other boy who was the other boy like George.

Q: Were you disturbed before the baby was born?

A: Yes, I was disturbed because my husband was teaching but they told him he was going to be very hard for him to be assistant professor. They say he wasn't good enough, but finally department has voted for the promotion. Other members had voted for the promotion and other members hadn't, so it was meant that finally majority had voted for the promotion.

Q: Did you worry about it?

A: Yes.

Q: Why were you disturbed in Tyler Hall?

A: They put me like if I was crazy. Nurse took me upstairs in such a terrible way, such a thing, that I become crazy.

Q: You thought somebody was making things difficult for your husband?

A: That's another thing. [R.D. Laing says that mental illness in an individual is often the symptom of mental illness of the entire family and of the social surroundings of that family. I agree with R.D. Laing.]

Q: Did you feel the nurse and the doctor were trying to kill you?

A: I was trying to say that maybe I wasn't feeling well.

Q: Do you think your mind wasn't right when you came here?

A: Yes, that's right, I was very upset over everything, but for what I don't know.

Q: Do you remember you were screaming a lot?

A: Yes.

Q: Why were you screaming?

A: Because I wanted to go out.

Q: What's this place for?

A: They say this is for your nerves.

Q: Was there anything wrong with your head when you came here?

A: Yes, I feel better, but I don't know what's my husband and my two boys and I want to see them.

Q: Do you think you needed to come here?
A: No.
Q: Did you hear voices talking about you?
A: Yes, in the other building.
Q: What did they say?
A: They say same thing as I was saying, push and all those things.

Emotional Reaction (March 2, 1949)—Patient remains suspicious and temperamental. "I was already feeling strange things in the office. They said I should sign a paper Mercedes Precioso Ugarte and they take my bag, my rings, the watch."

March 9—Since the last note patient has shown improvement. She has quieted down considerably. The wet sheet packs were discontinued. But patient was distressed when she was transferred to Hall Three. She became restless again, demanding her discharge. Patient said: "I was sick in the head. I was thinking about things." She recalls that she thought her boy was dead, and everybody was watching them, even the nurses.

March 13—Patient showing better judgment. Was seen conversing with the husband who wished to take her away; her things were packed after a short interview in which patient was appreciative for what had been done and expressed opinion that she developed better judgment, and she left in his care. They were planning to take the train north for Hanover. Condition upon discharge: recovered.

Opinions of the Staff—Dr. Gross: She is described as always having been sensitive, suspicious, and excitable. She started to show mental symptoms with birth of the baby. Auditory hallucinations, delusion of persecution. Perhaps you could call her a manic excitement. Noisy, irritable. She was concerned about the promotion of her husband. Was that the cause of her excitement? I don't know. I think this is a delirium of postpartum psychosis. I looked in the book to find out what class this would be here, and they don't have any special diagnosis of that kind. I would just leave her in paranoid type, postpartum psychosis, if such a diagnosis exits.

Dr. Holly: I had little doubt about the diagnosis until she made a rather interesting statement in which she said that in the past there have been periods when she was quite happy and quite depressed. Emotionally she is an unstable individual, not delirious, rather more a Manic-Depressive type of reaction.

Mr. Czatt: There is no doubt she is a suspicious individual. It was very hard for her to understand the sudden change on the part of people she thought were her friends, due to the lack of support for her husband's promotion; difficult to overestimate the impact of that. He shouldn't have, but the husband discussed it with her. Then there is the strangeness of the hospital and the fact also that she was afraid her child was going to be some sort of monster because of the congenital heredity. [Yes, she was told by family relations that her children might turn out to be monsters. George came out fine. Me, I'm not so sure.] *All this combined with the Spanish Civil War was being fought in her mind. She felt nurses and doctors were investigating them, questioning their loyalty and their right to have a place in the community.* [Mr., not Dr, Czatt, I think had the most astute and accurate diagnosis. My created Memory tells me he was a holocaust-survivor.]

Dr. Peladeau: A lot of things enter into this picture. First her tendency to extreme reactions. The fact that she went through the Civil War, conflicts about her own relatives and inner self and people in her environment. She made a definite transference of her fears from the War to her own mental state. She was under a great deal of pressure for several months before the child was born. The husband was also under pressure. It is interesting to note that at one point when she was being put in pack she jumped on one of the nurses and accused her of being intimate with her husband. Apparently there is some jealousy; whether she is projecting her former feelings about her husband, I don't know. This is the picture of a Manic and also strong paranoid coloring—makes you think more of a schizoid-affective sort of explosion. For the purposes of diagnosis, I believe I would be willing to leave her in the group of Manic sort of upset. If she is going to have future upsets, they might quite likely be more schizoid.

Dr. O'Neil: I thought she had a definite delirium, but Dr. McKenna said in his letter that she could be dissuaded from these beliefs quite readily; that doesn't sound like delirium. She said in the hospital she did not sleep, and said she was blue and depressed. I am inclined more toward Manic than postpartum delirium.

Dr. Elliot: It is difficult to evaluate this person in the particular time we are living. I imagine that a good number of newly arrived immigrants from Europe would be in a state of wonderment as to what was going to happen to them, especially when the family believes they are all secure and then people want to dismiss the husband. She is a rather hot-headed Spanish girl. [Thanks, Dr. Elliot, for your scientific appraisal.] *I have a hard time trying to decide what is normal and what is abnormal. There is this marked paranoid element throughout her whole performance, thinking that people were spies and that the nurse in the ward was her husband's former girlfriend, her aggressiveness. In view of her statements here, it would be proper to put in the affective group of emotional disturbances and call her a Manic. I am almost as suspicious of her as she is of others in that I can't satisfy myself that she is well, yet one has to give her the benefit of the doubt; I wouldn't be a bit surprised if she had further episodes.*

Tentative Diagnosis—Manic-Depressive Psychosis. Manic. [These assessments tell me as much or more about the psychiatric profession of the fifties than about my mom. But then again, at least some of what we are is what people think of us.]

Letter from Francisco Ugarte to Dr. Elliot, March 4, 1949—
[Francisco Ugarte is a missing link here. He is "the informant." Much of this report comes from what he told the doctors about my mom's history—a man suffering from the odd behavior of a crazy wife, a man determined to do the right thing but at the same time disturbed, even resentful, that the mother of his children could not be more normal. What they did not know is that Francisco was as crazy as she was, or maybe more.]

Dear Dr. Elliot:

With reference to the patient Mrs. Mercedes P. Ugarte, my wife, I plan to visit her on Sunday, March 6, and if possible I would like that you inform me of her case, or let me know in writing.

In the meantime, as of possible interest for her treatment, I have received today her first letter in Spanish, which I am translating below:

My dearest: Here I am where you left me. Apparently you, or whoever it may be, thought that this is the best place for me. I doubt it. But anyway, if in the end we get together again, the four of us or more (it is always better more than less), as we always wanted, I shall be the happiest woman in the world, as I have always been before this big mess and confusion that is not clear in my mind. But, darling, there is one thing for sure, and that is that my mind is completely firm and sure. Only that which surrounds me is confused and abnormal.

I received your letter of the 27th, and you state that you are sending me my traveling bag and another thing by mail which I hope they will give me within a few days. How anxious I am to be with you and speak normally of all this. Tell me about George. Tell me if he loves me and if he remembers me. How anxious I am to embrace you two! And tell me how is Michael. When I see him again he will probably have changed very much and he will be bigger. Darling, write me every day, and I will also. Goodbye, darling, I hope to see you soon. Love. Mercedes.

I hope you can give me reassuring news.

Sincerely,
Francisco Ugarte

For me, the son of Francisco and Mercedes, it's hard not to feel something very sharp in my gut when I read this letter. The anamnesis ends with a handwritten list of Mercedes Ugarte's possessions dated Feb. 25, 1949, when she was admitted, exactly nine days after I was born:

Coat (blue), loafers (brown), handkerchiefs (probably silk), corduroy (blue) coat, sleeve torn out when she came over (not here), nightgown (not here).

"Not here." Like my mom herself. And like my memory of some of those things. But some are palpable to me now well over fifty years later. The list goes on: *blue knit bed-jacket, silk bed jacket, blue silk nightgown, white silk nightgown, pink flowers, sanitary belt, blue slippers, small mirror, nylon hairbrush, lipstick, powder puff, panties, ballpoint pen, tweezers, toothbrush, comb, wristwatch, wedding ring, ring with white stone.*

The smell and feel of my mom's stuff emanated from those worn pages of the anamnesis. I swore I was breathing a remote past—when I was nine days old.

Chapter Two

Somewhere between New Hampshire and Vermont

She was forty-six, I was ten. She was sick, and I had no idea what kind of sickness it was. Dad would drive my older brother and me to visit her, a sixty-mile trip from Dartmouth College to the sanatorium in Glencliff, New Hampshire. It was the late spring of 1959, and I remember our family car was a mid-fifties tan-colored Chevy Bel Air with fins, a smooth comfortable ride through rolling hills. I had the backseat to myself. The greenery of New Hampshire surrounded the car, glacial lakes and low-elevation mountains with exotic names that rhymed: Sunapee, Winnipesaukee, Moosilauke. Even at age ten, the names of those mountains and lakes rattled off my tongue like they had always been in my life. I grew up in the midst of green forests, pines, white birches, and maples, so tall, and I was so short. Although I was usually a fidgety boy, always on the move, as I rode in the car I felt safe, uncharacteristically still on these trips, happy to be on my way to see my poor sick mom. My mother had tuberculosis; she was a patient at Glencliff sanatorium.

I don't think Glencliff will ever reopen as a TB sanatorium. In 1970 it became—what else?—a home for the elderly. Before those trips, they kept calling me back to the hospital in Hanover for tests—the results were not to the doctors' liking. My father and brother were fine, but not me. I didn't know it then, but Mercedes may have transmitted her sickness to me. None of that turned out to be important because I never showed any symptoms.

She had been diagnosed with a sickness not like a cold, or a sore throat, or the measles, all of which I had gone through. It was something else. I had no idea what was going on, just that my mom had to leave us for a while because she had TB or pleurisy (whatever that was) or both. I remember she had been skiing and had gotten a cold that landed her in bed for several days. Then we were all in the Mary Hitchcock Memorial Hospital in Hanover, waiting to be tested for a disease I believed harmless because that's what they kept telling me. But I didn't see much of her in the hospital. Mamá would be back in no time, they said, and our family would be whole again.

Not that it ever was. I wasn't sure she loved me. She rarely touched me. I don't remember a hug from her, although I'm sure she must have smothered me with motherly warmth at one time or another. It's frustrating that I can't remember being in her arms, cuddling, tickling, or caressing. How could a Spanish woman of a certain age and disposition not show a mother's affection? She was the most lively and dramatic woman I have ever known. After all, women from Spain are mothers by design, or so we are led to believe. Spanish people at times refer to Spain as *la madre patria* (the mother-fatherland), but there is no oxymoron here. Your mother is everything—your sustenance, your well-being, your responsibility, your identity, and your lord-guide. Womanly and manly. My mom played out that contradictory stereotype. But it also led to her demise.

On the trips to Glencliff I was content, because I thought my mom would be uncharacteristically affectionate when I saw her. Surely it was the northern New England beauty. Also that comfortable Chevy Bel Air. A pleasing ride to see my mom was making me happy. While my father was doing all he could to keep things as steady and quotidian as possible—cooking, cleaning, doing all the things Mercedes was responsible for—I sensed (then and now) her absence was difficult for him. There was something missing in our home, something we had gotten used to and was now absent, and that "something" did not come back into my life until Mercedes was in her eighties and I in my fifties.

Glencliff was at a higher elevation than Hanover, at the southern tip of the White Mountains. In those days the medical doctrine specified that exposure to fresh cold air was conducive to a cure of tuberculosis. So I suppose some people thought the climate of Glencliff was New Hampshire's equivalent to

Albuquerque, New Mexico, known as an important center for curing TB. But how are those two climates comparable? New Mexico is more like my mother's region, La Mancha (today Castilla-La Mancha), with its dryness, craggy mountains, vineyards, cliffs and mesas with occasional buildings on top: in La Mancha castles or churches, in New Mexico Native American shrines. Glencliff is not wine country, but it might be a good healthy place to recover from tuberculosis. What I have difficulty understanding is how the humidity of Glencliff could be conducive to the cure of TB. Then again, those who built the Glencliff Sanatorium at the turn of the twentieth century—no doubt hearty New Englanders with good intentions—probably did not have the dry climates of the Hispanic world in mind. Their eyes were more focused on the Swiss Alps and the healing capacities of Thomas Mann's *Magic Mountain*.

When we arrived, my father found parking with no difficulty; he wanted to be as close to the sanatorium as possible so that Mercedes could see me from her window. I was not allowed in the Glencliff convalescent home. They told me it was risky; I was too young. I was more susceptible to contagion than adults or adolescents like my brother. But my brother was just five years older than me, so today their rationale is questionable. I suspect it had more to do with the fact that the tests for TB I had taken were not conclusive, or perhaps they showed there was a possibility of my developing my mother's illness. In any case, I had to stay in the car. It was parallel parked alongside the building, in front of a spacious porch with outdoor chairs for patients and relatives. No one was sitting on that porch. It occurred to me that my mom might come out on the porch to see me, but that didn't happen. I watched my dad and brother walk away from the car; they both had their heads down as if they weren't looking forward to the visit. I sensed their concern, their preoccupation for my sick mom. They entered the building and disappeared. But the cushions of the Chevy Bel Air and my own boyish imagination trying to escape from the sobriety of the moment allowed me to forget them at least for a little while. All I had to do was entertain myself in the car and wait to see if I could get a glimpse of my mom.

I've seen some photos of Glencliff Sanatorium when it was first built, as well as today's Glencliff home for the elderly. The two structures could not be more different. The new building is all on one floor and semi-circular. It has that institutional look that tries to evade the reality of its *institutionalness*. In the new Glencliff, gone is the old-time look of the sanatorium of 1959: a red brick building, several stories with an attic and a basement. Dormers on the top floor with windows at the basement level. I read that it only housed about fifty patients in those days. At the time I thought it was palatial, but I see now it was probably only around thirty meters wide and from roof to ground around fifteen. As I look at the image on my computer I am surprised by the accuracy of my recollection, as if the cyber-world has verified what I was feeling as a ten-year-old boy. Memory, you have not let me down, at least not in this case.

    I recall several visits to Glencliff, some with my brother, some without. He was a teenager at that time and had his own life, friends, sports, parties; I did not see him as frequently as I would have liked, and I'm sure my mother was disappointed when he did not accompany me and my dad on those trips. The visit I remember most vividly is a day it rained. I was alone in the car while my brother and father were visiting my mother. Were they in her room? In a lounge? Could they have been in a cafeteria? Those are questions I ask now but not at the time. I entertained myself by watching the raindrops hit the car windows on all sides. I created races between the drops from the top of the window to the bottom. Sometimes several drops at once. I loved the drops that started out slow and suddenly slid down to the bottom of the window, beating all the others that had started faster and with more determination. But those slow drops did not always win. Sometimes they didn't go the distance, or they didn't move at all. But that was ok, because there were always others willing to enter the race. I cheered for the ones that started slow and ended up winning. The track and field of raindrops kept my interest for what must have been a long time; I wasn't bored, or sad, or restless, or scared. I was oblivious to everything except the raindrops, their movement, their different shapes and sizes.

    But the rain stopped. That same afternoon the sun made its presence known: a sunny and green spring day, the kind that gives people in New Hampshire a thrill after months of snow and below-zero temperatures. Spring takes a while to arrive, but when it does, there's no more need for Prozac: lilacs, tulips, and a variety of wildflowers in all their colors cure what ails you. I saw her from one of the windows. She smiled. It was her: dark hair curling up at neck level, bright brown eyes, a soft mouth, lips red, a hint of glimmer, and most of all, anticipation in her expression, as if to say, *There you are, Miguel, mi Miguelito. Don't worry, I'll be home soon.*

Then her attention turned from outside the window to inside. My dad and brother were probably there with her, maybe a doctor too, or a nurse. Seeing her was reassuring to me. It turned into a nice day, so I got out of the car and strolled over to the woods surrounding the hospital. There was something like a path through the pines and spruces. The woods were laced with flowers peeking up at me from the wild grass in the path. I was looking for buttercups and black-eyed Susans. I picked them up and tore away the petals and said to myself, "She loves me, she loves me not," and I would repeat the first half of that line with every petal I removed from the flower. And so the superstition goes, if the last petal ended with "she loves me," the truth is she loved me. I never ended with "she loves me not," because I just didn't want it to end that way. A ten-year-old knows how to manipulate the will of nature. If you step on the crack that will break your mother's back, there is always something you can do to remedy the situation—go back, jump over to the next one, tell yourself you didn't step on it. In my case I knew just what to do. Unlike stepping on cracks by mistake, tearing a petal off a flower was something wholly within my control. Because after I had seen my mom smile at me through the windowpane, there was no doubt: the black-eyed Susans told me my mom loved me.

Memory, allow me if you can, to return to the day I was born. I want to go back ten years before those trips to Glencliff—February 16, 1949. Just a week later my mom ended up in another institution, this one in Brattleboro, Vermont. Here is a memory I cannot possibly recall, although some claim to know firsthand what happened during their infancy. In my case, I know through secondary sources that my mom was in a "Retreat" in Brattleboro. I received textual proof in the form of an official record of her stay. But maybe a story of something that happened to a family member told by someone else gives it an aura of unwarranted importance. Is Memory an aura? If so, for me it makes Memory all the more real.

I think in some ways my mother was predisposed to institutionalization: boarding schools in Spain and four hospital stays in the U.S., albeit for short times. The hospital complex in Brattleboro was built in the mid-1800s, and it was known in its origin as the Vermont Asylum for the Insane. The proverbial "funny farm," in all its political incorrectness. The Brattleboro Mental Institution of the 1950s, or the Brattleboro Retreat, prided itself on being one of the most advanced hospitals for the mentally ill. Again, with the aid of cyber information I am informed that it was unique in its humane treatment of patients—no barbed-wire fences or padded cells. Its "electroconvulsive therapy" (shock treatment) was used sparingly. Good thing, because I surmise that my mother may have been a candidate. On the other hand, they did not spare the use of icepacks.

My mother's mental illness had many different phases and degrees, and the hospital record along with my memory of what Mercedes told me about it makes it real. This episode, just days after I was born, was pivotal. Family members of her generation related to me on several occasions that my mother had always suffered from *ataques de nervios* (nervous attacks or hysterics). What I was told when I was growing up is that my birth had triggered an episode sufficiently severe that my father was advised to take her to the Brattleboro hospital. I have no idea when I found out about this. But I do recall it made me sad, or it made me think my mother was special, and not in a good way.

For years I had the impression that Mercedes was in the Brattleboro Retreat for several months or longer, but now I know she was there only eighteen days. My mistaken impression tells me how much of an impact the experience had, despite the fact that it constituted only a few weeks of her life. She said so herself, and my father confirmed it many times. The Brattleboro experience became part of the intimate family lore, even though outside the family we were reluctant to talk about it. My friends made fun of the place as they circled their ears with their forefingers and crossed their eyes. I didn't tell them my mom had been there. I didn't tell them she'd been cuckoo.

As years went by, she talked about her stay in the Retreat, and her memory was not a fond one. She talked about being subdued, about cruel nurses. Ice, ice, cold, freezing cold all around her small body; she thought she was dying. As she told us about it, she made a face as if she was about to cry, her cheeks and forehead crumpled up, her eyes squinted. She accompanied those expressions with hand gestures, at times encircling her face as if to frame it for a photo or a painting. My mother was melodramatic to the core, and most of the time those who knew her took what she said in stride. But when she talked about Brattleboro, some listened and empathized. For me the empathy grew with age. When I was younger, all that drama, often manipulative, feeling empathy for Mercedes was not easy.

I searched for references to Brattleboro in a memoir she was writing. At the time of her move from West Lebanon, New Hampshire, to Columbia, Missouri, in 1997, I found pieces of that text—notebooks and a few pages here and there, some written on two-by-five-inch inserts from old copies of *Time* magazine; she used those scraps of paper as note cards. She told anyone listening, or appearing to listen, that she titled her text *Los Años Después* (The Years After), which I thought may have referred to the years after she had been hospitalized. I also, in my self-centeredness, conjured the possibility that the years after meant the time after I was born. But I know now that's wrong. When I asked her what she meant by "The Years After," she was coy, like a famous writer who doesn't want to give away the main idea of a provocative story. As with that famous writer, you suspect they don't know either; they just like the way the words sound. What I do know is that the Brattleboro experience set off something always lingering in the darkness of her mind, filled with treachery and pain. Today I know that the years after were the years (forty of them) after my father's suicide.

Part II

Chapter Three

Going Back to a Time You Cannot Know

Some tell us that mental illness shows up after the trauma of a difficult childhood: cruel nuns in a convent school, an abusive father, an accident, a horrific memory. Judgments like these come to us out of necessity, from an urge to explain something inexplicable. It's difficult, if not impossible, to accept that the behavior has no cause or reason. I know that my mom suffered at times from mental illness; she herself felt sometimes that she would sink into a hole and never come up again. I heard her say this many times when she was visibly distraught, or when she wanted me to see her wounds: "It's a sinking thing, Miguel." Or as she put it, "Eess a seenkeen theen." And she repeated "seenkeen theen" several times, like she was singing a blues song. The image of my mother sinking into a chasm of her own mind has been with me for as long as I can remember.

It's undeniable, at least for me, that traumas in childhood have something to do with mental illness. My mom had both traumas *and* a family history of mental illness. Her early years transpired long ago in a land far away from where she gave birth to me. I can only understand my mother's far away land (both in space and time) if I make use of what she and others told me about it. But as someone who has been no stranger to libraries or archives, I've also relied on information gathered from written histories, and recorded accounts of that childhood land in which she lived. I'm a professor of Spanish language and culture, so, as I've been thinking for a long time, I feel not only an urge but an obligation to try to put her life together. Will all of it be "right"? No, in a narrow sense, but an incorrect memory is still a memory and it tells us something about the person remembering and even about the things remembered. I can hear my mom giving me advice about all this: "*Miguel, esto puede ser verdad y no haber pasado.*" (Miguel, this could be true and not have happened.) Yes, Mom you got that right, so here goes. What follows is true but didn't happen, or it's not true but surely did happen.

My mother's mother, Marina Ugarte Cristobal, died in 1918 at the age of twenty-nine, when my mom was only five. Marina Ugarte was one of many casualties of the so-called Spanish influenza, a misnomer since it was a pandemic that spread from France into Spain and Portugal made its way to the Americas and somehow managed to creep back into Europe. When her mother died, Mercedes had no inkling of pandemics, or plagues, or infestations, but I can imagine that for a girl of five with a little sister and an infant brother, the death of your mom brings on lots of trauma. When Mercedes spoke to me of her mother, it sounded like she was describing a dream—a bad one at times, and at others a good one.

My mom's mother, Marina was married to a rising author and editor, Artemio Precioso García (my grandfather), who had cast aside the family's assumptions that he would continue in the successful entrepreneurial line of his father, José Precioso Roche, a landowner from Hellín in La Mancha who had invested in metals and lumber. José died in 1903 when Artemio was thirteen. Marina's mother and father were from the Basque Country.

Artemio Sr., Aspiring writer. circa 1912

Her lover and husband, Artemio Precioso García, was an intrepid and ambitious writer who, when my mom was born, was not as much interested in the family enterprises as in literature, politics, and the arts. His courtship with Marina went smoothly, although problems came after the romance. What I do not know for sure is what Marina, a girl born in Brussels, the eldest child of a mining engineer from the Basque Country, was doing in Hellín. Her mother was from Aragón, and her name was Micaela, hence my name, Michael in the U.S. and Miguel in Spain. I surmise (with little documentary evidence available) that their presence in that town of La Mancha was due to my paternal grandfather's (Javier's) pecuniary ambitions. By pecuniary ambitions, I mean he was probably looking for useful minerals in Hellín, an area known for its sulfur deposits. It could also be that my dad's dad Javier had something to do with the construction of a dam in that area, the Balsa de Capote. My dad was the only member of the Ugartes born in Hellín, and that's where he met my mom for the first time.

But because of the influenza, Artemio Precioso's marriage to Marina Ugarte Cristobal lasted only six years. In those six years, he was busy establishing a name for himself as a local writer and journalist. He loved her dearly, he says in an unpublished autobiography (*Autobiografía*); he thought she was "one of the most beautiful, affectionate, and generous women [he had] ever known." But he also admits he was not a good husband: sanguine, moody, unaffectionate, capable of not saying a single word at a family dinner. He says he was also prone to jealousy with no cause. As she lay dying, his wife Marina pleaded with him not to marry again, because a second marriage would make everyone miserable, all this, according to his autobiography written shortly after the end of the civil war, a manuscript that his son Artemio and my cousin Amado have kept for many years. Here my grandfather also confirmed something that my mother had told me long ago: Marina Ugarte was pregnant when she died. But that child did not survive.

Mercedes' father was an impetuous man by all accounts; he did not heed his first wife's dying advice. It took him some twenty-four months to marry again. Indeed, the family of his second wife, Amelia, was vehemently opposed for the very reason Marina asked him not to marry again: his temperament was not of the marrying kind. The *Autobiografía*, as he titled it, goes into details about the machinations he had to go through to get the family to agree to the second marriage, something that I recall was seen in my family as a mark of his passionate love and romanticism. My mom told me so.

But after reading the autobiography, it's difficult to come to that conclusion. He admits that the second marriage was something of an act of defiance against the family's disapproval. What's more, in his life narrative—remarkably and disturbingly honest—the tone is often vindictive. My mother's father was a man who had an ax to grind, for just reasons or not, against the many people who had done him wrong, financially, professionally, and morally. Of this I can be sure; as I look into my mother's craziness, it's clear to me now that she shared many of her father's traits. The autobiography was written while he was under house arrest. In confinement he brooded about everything that had happened to him, understandably so. He describes himself as a man whose democratic ideals could do little or nothing to counter the traditionalism, authoritarianism, and bad faith that prevailed in his day. Indeed, widower of Marina Ugarte, husband of Amelia, and father of Mercedes, Marina, Artemio Jr., Soledad, Maruja, and Amelia, Artemio Precioso was a man who took the opportunity of his house arrest in Isso to come to terms with his resentments through writing.

But not always. Artemio had lots of good words for those he loved and respected. In one of the rare mentions of my mother, he not only speaks adoringly of his first wife, whom he lost way too young, he also extends her qualities to Mercedes, Marina, and Artemio Jr., "three exemplary children worthy of their mother for their charms, physical health, and the purity of their altruistic sentiments." He is remembering his children in their infancy as well as in their adulthood, adults who, by the time of this writing—1944—had made many life choices. Mercedes had married an aspiring young diplomat (my father), Marina had stayed in Hellín to marry a fine gentleman whose photo in Republican military uniform was in her possession for many years, and Artemio Jr., politically idealistic, was committed

Back row: Artemio Sr., possibly Amparo, Marina (Mercedes' mom), Mercedes in front, circa 1916

to the creation of a better world.

As my grandfather wrote his life story he was aware of his own renown. A man who was mostly absent from my mother's life due to his commitments, but who, at the same time, had a lasting effect on her. There is portrait of him painted by a well-known artist of that day, Julio Romero de Torres, that now hangs in the Instituto de Estudios Albacetenses (a public library specializing in all things from La Mancha and Albacete) due to the generosity of my cousin Amado, who owned the original.

To have posed for a portrait by Romero de Torres is ample proof of my grandfather's importance in Spanish society of the twenties and thirties. Listen to what his biographer, Francisco Linares, says about him:

Autographed copy of charcoal portrait of Artemio Sr.; (artist unknown) circa 1932

> Few people live a life of such intensity and liberty as Artemio Precioso, despite everything and everyone. The 1920s [in Spain] marked a time of great agitation, a time in which this man—lawyer, journalist, businessman, gourmet, inveterate traveler, and definitely *bon vivant*—spread his wings. His bigger-than-life personality captivated people who encircled him at the same time as it was the object of scorn for others, predominantly the right wing. (Francisco Linares, ed., *Españoles en el destierro*, my translation).

Yes, Artemio Precioso García was a *bon vivant*, as well as a talented man. My mom told me he won a poetry contest in Hellín in what's known as the *Juegos Florales* (Floral Games); today we might call this a kind of poetry slam celebrated in many parts of Spain and Europe that has its origins in ancient Rome, a competition to decide who is the most clever wordsmith of a given community. I know the poem because my mom recited it to me many times. It was a sonnet about Christ on the cross suffering and dying for the world's vileness. The last lines, though, are filled with redemption, hope for humanity in the figure of Mary Magdalene—the chaste prostitute—weeping at the foot of the cross:

>Muerto en la cruz, los brazos extendidos,
>han perdonado la maldad ajena,
>bajo el áureo fulgor de su melena
>sus ojos se ven ya desfallecidos.
>
>Los astros en el cielo están dormidos
>y en la tierra ni un leve rumor suena,
>sólo bajo la cruz la Magdalena
>desgrana silenciosa sus gemidos.
>
>Señor, si en esta lucha envilecida
>me crucifica el odio del contrario,
>dadme una Magdalena, que llore
>un poco de amor en mi calvario.

(My translation:
Dead on the cross, arms extended,
evil is forgiven.
Beneath the shimmering aura of his crown,
his eyes are about to close.

The stars hovering above are asleep,
and on earth not a sound.
At his feet, Mary Magdalene weeps.

Lord, in this life's heinous battle,
as the hate of my enemies crucifies,
give me a Madeleine,
and relieve my agony with her tears of love.)

But neither my grandfather nor my mother was God-fearing in the traditional sense. This modern sonnet is more than anything a performance;

its powerful Christian message, comes to us via a comparison between Mary Magdalene, the saintly prostitute, to the pastry that bears her name. It is a captivating ode to the most spiritual of biblical women gone astray. Her presence assuages the devastation to humanity as a result of the crucifixion, and it reminds us that Christ forgave her. My grandfather's thoughtful evocation of a sense of sweetness reminds us that Proust's famous pastry, the madeleine, was and remains just as Spanish as French—Proust's spirit is everywhere including in this little town of Hellín. My mother loved madeleines, and I'm convinced (or I've convinced myself) that she loved them for her remembrance of this "thing past": her father's sorrowfully sweet award-winning poem at the Floral Games of Hellín, Albacete, circa 1905.

Many years later, when dementia had just begun to take its toll on my mom's mind and body, she was able to recite this poem publicly in a coffee place in Columbia, Missouri. It was a poetry recital I had organized in which my graduate students would declaim and translate their favorite poems. I invited my mom, and she accepted the invitation with glee. I recall that at age eighty-one she bellowed out her father's words, her voice trembling. The tribute to Artemio Sr. came from the memory of his hardships, but it went beyond that. Like my grandfather, she was performing; she loved to be seen in public, and when people listened to her, she seemed happy. She had endured years of neglect before she moved to Missouri, speaking to herself, lots of nonsense, always gesticulating as if she were Violetta in *La Traviata*, while those around her (including me) looked at her as if she were the madwoman in the attic.

Mercedes declaiming her father's poem
Artisan Cafe, Columbia, Missouri
2002

I remember the looks she got in that coffee place. People seemed to admire the old woman declaiming a poem written by her father in the first decade of the twentieth century. Our audience was mostly made up of a coffee shop clientele unaware that their space was going to be invaded by a group of Spanish poetry students with their teacher and his one-foot-in-the-grave mother. But that old lady made them look up; she was the poetry recital's most enthusiastic participant. She declaimed from memory her father's sonnet to Mary Magdalene, and with the lines "*Señor . . . dame una magdalena . . .*" (Lord, give me a madeleine. . .) her voice rose and her face contorted. I suspected that perhaps she had a hidden religious streak all along, but that suspicion was short-lived. My mom always loved the drama.

Back to Hellín; there was drama in that town too. Mercedes' mother fell in love with the author of that sonnet about Christ's final moment with Mary Magdalene, and he with her. I'm told it was a *flechazo* (Cupid's arrow), a maximum attraction that, regardless of the family's disapprobation, was typically passionate like any young romance defying family and society. Alas, their love didn't last the eternity it promised. Marina died too young. Although my mother's recollection of her was sparse, it had a certain dreamlike quality. How else does a girl of five remember her mom? Mercedes did remember, however—dream or nightmare—when she was led to her mother's open coffin and coaxed by servants and family to give her mother a final kiss. She related this to me years later: she wanted to stay by her mother's side, but the adults wouldn't let her. One of the servants taking care of the children took her away as she screamed, "*Mamá, Mamá.*"

All this takes me to something within my lifetime, another funeral, my father's in Hanover, New Hampshire, 1969. I see my mother dressed in black, a gauze veil over her face. Her eyes tell anyone who dares to look at her that she is in a daze. Contrary to the suggestions of the good people at the Rand Funeral Home in Hanover, my brother and I wanted the casket open so Mother could have tangible evidence he was dead. She had thought she was the victim of a terrible deception. In her mind, my father had not killed himself, he had abandoned her; he just took off to God knows where. It was his way of divorcing or abandoning her, or so she believed. For the week after his suicide, I don't recall seeing her cry. She seemed more bewildered than grief-stricken. Given her state of shock, the open casket was a way of allowing her to see the truth for herself, or so we thought. I remember vividly that she approached the funeral altar where he lay in the casket, his nose pointed upward, his neck swollen, his face redder than normal. But despite all that, he was pretty much intact. It was Paco. The funeral home had done an excellent job in disguising the appearance of a grotesquely broken body that had leapt from a bridge over a 160-foot precipice. But in the long run, the open casket did not dissuade my mom from the idea—psychologists call it "ideation"—that my dad wasn't dead; he was hiding from her.

I wonder if the sight of my father lying in his coffin reminded Mercedes of her mother Marina fifty-one years earlier in Hellín: the open casket with people grieving around her. My mother was encouraged to kiss her mom, just as she was told to approach her husband's casket. I imagine that the wake in Hellín, like the one in Hanover, was attended by family members, friends of the deceased, important members of the community. In Hellín, there were servants at the funeral. That cry "*Mamá, Mamá*" comes back to haunt, a cry to which many probably reacted by sighing, *Pobrecita* (poor little girl). When I asked my mother, she told me she could not recall the room where her mother lay, the people around her, or if her sister and infant brother were with her. So I'll stay on my mother's refrain, "Could be true and not have happened."

I rely on another ethereal memory of her mother. This one is from her younger sister, Marina. My grandmother's namesake described it in a conversation with my mother many years later. Both were in their eighties, talking about their childhood in an ice cream place a few miles north of Alicante. My aunt recalled that their mother loved to play games with the two girls. She would stand on a chair and lift a spoon as high as she could reach and yell, *"Tocino del cielo"* (a custard dish similar to flan, literally the name of the dish means "bacon grease from the sky,"—but more poetically if not more accurately "manna from heaven"). The girls would reach for it, pretending the manna from heaven was falling all around them like gentle sweet rain. My mother said to her sister, "Marina, you can't remember that, you were too young." But my aunt Marina swore she remembered as if it were yesterday, their mom's voice laughing and singing, *"Tocino del cielo."* My mother was annoyed at the recollection, perhaps distraught that she did not remember: it couldn't have happened, but it was probably true. Moments of tenderness did not predominate Mercedes' memories of her childhood. She was always a bit jealous of her sister. If sister Marina remembered this, why didn't Mercedes?

Then there was Amparo, the maid; everyone remembered Amparo, my mom too, and she talked about her with sincere kindness. How could anyone not have felt something tender for the woman who became something of a stand-in mother to the three children of Artemio Precioso after the untimely death of his beautiful wife? And how could anyone in the family cast Amparo into oblivion? "Amparo" means protection, succor. Like virtually anyone growing up in the United States, my social and cultural registers have much to do with race relations (even in New Hampshire), and Amparo, to me, was not unlike the countless black female descendants of slaves I had read about or seen on TV, caretakers of rich white children. Like something out of a nineteenth-century European novel—all those saintly servant-peasants in Tolstoy—Amparo took care of Artemio Precioso's children with much devotion.

Amparo was a baker's daughter from Tobarra, province of Albacete, about eleven kilometers from Hellín. She was sent to serve the Precioso family as a live-in maid when she was in her teens, and that's where she stayed until she died. This was not uncommon in the Spain of that time. Many families could not afford to take care of and feed their children; sending the girls to serve a well-to-do family was a matter of survival. I know Amparo lived with my mom's sister's family from her adolescence to her death because my aunt Marina took care of her in her old age. Amparo was loyalty incarnate, "with a heart bigger than all of La Mancha," or so many of the descendants of José and Artemio Precioso told me. We all loved her. Even my mother, not known for her affection or understanding of people "below" her, had a soft spot for Amparo, her surrogate mom. We were her family. She never seemed to wish to go back to her "real" family in Tobarra, or at least that's what my mother and father said. Perhaps the truth lies elsewhere. In any case, when my grandmother died, Amparo must have taken over the care of the children. And later on, after all the hardship of the Civil War, when Mercedes and Paco returned to Hellín from the U.S. for the first time in sixteen years, I saw my mother embrace her in a way that surprised me. All my brother and I saw in the woman named Protection was a four-foot-something old lady who had a wart on her cheek that seemed to cover the entire side of her face. To us she was ugly, grotesque even; we didn't want to be near her. "¡Qué asco!" (gross, disgusting) my brother would say. "Ugly as sin." But the devil was nowhere to be found when Amparo was in the room, any room. When my brother said in English, "Ugly as sin," so the family would not understand, I went along with him. But we were utterly mistaken. The devil was no match for the generosity of Amparo emanating with such force, such beauty, that no doubt it made Lucifer arch his spine and head back to Hell. My brother hated our family obligation of kissing her, and I was influenced by his repulsion. But I recall that when I did kiss her out of obligation, I began to understand my mother's uncharacteristically loving embrace. Amparo's face was pleasant to the touch, wrinkly-soft, milky velvet, her smile unquestionably genuine. I have a feeling my brother was equally surprised, but we never talked about it. I don't know how old she was at the time; she seemed ancient. I don't think she knew how old she was either. For her it was a blessing to see that Paco and Mercedes had returned to their home with two darling boys (ages five and ten), *preciosos*, like their name.

After Mercedes' mother died, there were changes in the Precioso household. Within two years Artemio remarried. Amelia Precioso Lafuente was not only available, she had property and a connection to the family. She became the stepmother, and it was clear among members of the family that her relations with my grandfather were more functional than romantic. Years later, not only my mother but my father and other Preciosos compared La Mamá Amelia (as she was known to us) to the real mother, and Amelia could not compete. Indeed, the memory

Back: Artemio Sr.,
Front, left to right:
Marina, Mercedes, Mamá Amelia
(Artemio's second wife)
Circa 1928

of Marina was that of the genuine mother in every sense—pretty, soft, tender, young, and *encantadora* (enchanting). The fact that she died young made all those traits stand out. Still, unlike all those stereotypes about the mean stepmother, the intruder, the one who represents a bitter change in the family dynamic, Amelia performed her motherly duties with care. There were no complaints about her from Artemio's three children until she was unable to take care of herself in her later years, thus becoming a burden on the family.

My mother always spoke of her with affection. Her status as mother was consolidated with the birth of three of her own children, Maruja, Amelia, and

Soledad (Sole), all of whom my mom considered her own sisters, and that's how they were presented to my brother and me. They were our aunts, and Mamá Amelia was the closest thing to a grandparent we had. In a sense my mom had three mothers—Marina, Amparo, and Amelia—while at the same time, she had none. A motherless child at age five, despite the surrogates, she remained something of an orphan until her death. So many mothers—too many. All three combined added up to zero. But there's no denying she was also a child of privilege: her daddy was rich, and although her mother died when she was five, she had two surrogate moms, and one was good looking. Still, her father was by no means a model of fatherly engagement with his daughters. And his womanizing was known to just about everyone who knew him; he admits as much in his memoir. My mom told me he was always working, thinking, writing, ever engaged in his enterprises, and rarely near her. Despite the distance, however, my mom was very proud of her father.

As she and others tell his story, Hellín was not big enough for Artemio Precioso García. Madrid would be his destination; the capital of Spain was a center of urbanity and good taste to him, as well as to natural-born Manchegos itching to arrive at the big city. He was not a man who did what he was told. His defiance was rebellious but not in the Bohemian antibourgeois way, like all those youngsters and artists eager to act out against convention. Rather he was a man who knew the power of a *peseta*, and he would use that power to go his own way. With the money he inherited he went off to Madrid to launch several editorial endeavors and to write. At the time he had three children. The oldest was my mom who grew to live the cosmopolitan Madrid of the twenties and thirties; she loved the sophistication, the urbane manners, the "beautiful people" out for a walk in the Retiro Park—something like New York's Central Park. And my hunch is that, as the daughter of Artemio Precioso, people must have taken notice of her, if anything for the pricey and pretty things she was wearing. Indeed, it must have been exciting to be the daughter of a well-known public figure.

Now with the details of a history that was denied Spaniards for several decades by two dictators, Primero de Rivera and Franco, the public life of Artemio Precioso has reemerged. Even before the civil war, during the years of the first dictatorship in the 1920s, he had many difficulties all stemming from what some called his "Voltairian" sensibilities and his public determination to help create an enlightened society. As biographer Francisco

Linares says, he was a *bon vivant*, a freethinker, anticlerical (albeit not rabid), steadfastly Republican (meaning antimonarchist), and progressive regarding different forms of behavior and sexuality. He founded several publishing houses and paid his authors well. The most noteworthy writers of the day wrote for his literary enterprises. He wrote many popular short stories or novellas published individually and sold in kiosks, with titles like *The Virgin Wife, Double Passion, Why Do They Deceive*—"they" refers to women, not men—*When Love is Born, Pleasures and Crimes on Board*, and *Carmela's Triumph*. This last was about a lesbian couple dealing with the prohibitions of their day and their feelings of culpability. But through their own ingenuity and concealment of their behavior, they are able to depend on their rich husbands and enjoy (physically and otherwise) their own company happily ever after. The popular genre he cultivated was called in those days the *novela de kiosko* (kiosk novel)—short novels sold at an affordable price in kiosks.

What my mother remembered about her father was hazy, and many times when I asked about him she became sad or evasive. But what I do know is that the entire family moved to Paris in 1927 and lived there for several years. The youngest, Sole, was born there. Like a plethora of prominent writers of that time, my grandfather was forced out of the country. The root cause of his ouster was his criticism of the dictatorship, but the immediate impetus for leaving was financial. He had lost several lawsuits leveled against him alleging libel or some form of infraction. Apparently, he'd violated the sensibilities of supporters of the regime, many of them politicians who were the strong man's sycophants. Others were high military officials, and still others the gatekeepers of decency, usually clerics eager to include his works on the Index Librorum Prohibitorum, the infamous list of prohibited books compiled by the Catholic Church.

Exile has its ups and downs, and Artemio's was no different. The downs are hard: the person in exile is torn from nation and community, a price much too costly for speaking one's mind. But it's difficult to deny that for some there are advantages: a new horizon, different sensibilities that might spark innovative ideas. Another benefit for him and his family was that it allowed his daughters not only to see Paris, but to live it. Indeed, my mom benefited a great deal from all these Voltairian influences, as well as from her experiences in Paris, the place some have called the capital of Europe.

What we don't find in the writings by my grandfather, or in the ones about him is much discussion of his six children. My mom had fond recollections of her life in France. There she learned to speak French, and she never forgot it. In fact, she used her French language proficiency to show the world her worth, even in inappropriate situations. When she was introduced to someone rich or important, she would address them in French regardless of their ability to carry on a conversation in that language. It was her one-upmanship: "*Vous connaissez Paris? Ou là là. C'est une ville si belle.*" (Do you know Paris? Ou là là, such a beautiful city). And she would say this with such aplomb, albeit her heavy Spanish accent, that her non-French-speaking interlocutor could do nothing but blush or smile, mumbling something like, "Um, no, I've never been there. Is that what you asked?" And the poor schmuck—an administrator, a doctor, someone in a position to compete for a higher post in a small Ivy-League town—would have to admit that my mother had won this (petty) battle that he didn't even want to wage.

It was in France also that she received the relatively little formal education offered to her. From Paris the children were sent to Hendaye on the Spanish-French border, perhaps to be closer to Spain, since Artemio's intentions of remaining in France were uncertain. Another possibility is that financing an apartment for a family of eight in the City of Light is not easy for anyone who has just lost a fortune. Yet, according to biographer Francisco Linares, as founder of La Novela de Hoy, Artemio continued his literary career in Paris with some financial success. He always seemed to land on his feet. The tragic part came later.

My mom often said she enjoyed being a student, not as much for the studies as for the opportunities to meet boys. "*Guapos, altos, rubios* (Handsome, tall, blond)." Need we add rich? She kept a note that one of these boys had written her, and she recited it years later, not only to me but to anyone within earshot. It was a mildly erotic poem:

Tus pantorrillas Mercedes, son dos columnas perfectas.
Sostienen, y no me pegues,
un montón de cosas hermosas.
(Your calves, Mercedes, are two perfect columns.
They are pillars—please don't slap me—
holding up a heap of pretty things.)

From her father's writings, both fiction and nonfiction, I suspect don Artemio was also taken by the calves of pretty women, considering all the shapely legs that figure in his stories.

Many years later, when she moved to Missouri, I introduced her to many people—friends, colleagues, students—and what they seemed to react to most positively was her mischievous references to sex, however benign. I am convinced today that she got that from her dad. Artemio Precioso was known for testing the limits of decency; his writing allured readers for that reason. It was always a commercial success, and from his many prologues to the short novels he published, it's clear he was eminently proud of his economic prowess. My mom was proud of him for this too. Today I surmise that my mom's predilection for naughty behavior came at least in part from the fact that my grandfather made a good living by writing borderline prurient stories that people consumed either happily or secretly or both.

The word used at that time for the kind of erotic sensibility that Artemio Precioso was engaged in was *sicalíptico*, difficult to define, impossible to translate accurately. The easy definition is "erotic," but it's more than that. It has to do with something odd, out of the ordinary, at the margins of traditional sexual norms—perhaps "kinky" with a pseudoscientific resonance. To write of these things in Primo de Rivera's Spain was to take risks, even though the dictator himself was well known for womanizing. In my grandfather's writing there are suggestions of masturbation (only suggestions, mind you), characters attracted to people of the same sex (at times ridiculed at times taken seriously) nymphomania, and adultery, some leading to tragic ends. I heard my mom say the word *sicaplíptico* referring to her father's writing many times. When I first heard her say it I thought she had made it up in her mischievous attempt to be alluring and naughty. Studying my grandfather's life and work, I realize that my mom's assessment was on the mark, evidence for what many of us suspected—that the Spain of the twenties and thirties was a preamble to what happened after the death of Franco, not only democracy but more importantly, loosened sexual morays.

When I became intensely interested in her life in Spain, I asked my mom to tell me about her father, and she obliged. She would tell me he was the victim of envious people. She was unabashedly proud of his having been such a prominent cultural figure; she often insisted he was a dear friend of several of the most canonical writers in the country. One of those, Vicente Blasco Ibáñez, became well known in the U.S. for having written *The Four Horsemen of the Apocalypse*, adapted into a 1921 film starring Rudolph Valentino. After their move to the States, I remember that my mother and father went to the 1961 film version of the novel, starring Glenn Ford and Yvette Mimieux. My mom, an avid movie-goer, loved it, while my dad said Hollywood had turned one of Blasco Ibáñez's lesser novels into something even lesser.

I began to check into the life of my mother's father on my own, all the time wondering what effect this highly visible man had on his loved ones, especially my mom. I found that there were many denunciations of my grandfather's writing for its licentiousness, a few of which landed him in court before his move to Paris. One of his short novels, *El légamo de la tragedia* (The Mire of Tragedy), led to several lawsuits. This one may have been the one that ruined him. It was about a young man who kills his estranged lover out of jealousy, indeed a "dirty tragedy." One of the characters is a woman theater critic, Josefina, who becomes very fond of Anita (the young victim of the crime), much to the chagrin of Anita's lover; there is a less-than-subtle suggestion that the theater critic is erotically attracted to her. Josefina is described by my grandfather as something between man and woman: "Josefina knew she was not a woman, although she was not a man either. She believed that her flings with men wouldn't last. In the deepest reaches of her being, she knew she was more male than female, so for that reason she had the ability to open herself to the attraction, gratitude, and passion of many pretty young women" (my translation).

This novel, like many of those either written or published by Mercedes' father was attacked by the conservative establishment. One of the detractors was a woman who felt that Artemio Precioso was alluding to her in his fictional character Josefina in light of an interview with Artemio in the form of a prologue to the novel. Asked if the events in his novel were real, Artemio suggested coyly that his novel was indeed based on a real incident: "I offer reality in my writings," he wrote. "No matter how much we use imagination, reality always appears as a fierce beast." The fierce beast in this case was the lovesick killer, but it also could have been the female/male theater critic who had convinced the man's love object that he wasn't worth much, surely in order to keep her for herself. The woman who felt she was portrayed in the novel sued the author for libel, and she won. My mother was in her early teens at the time.

Years later I heard many arguments between Mercedes and Paco having to do with Artemio Precioso. My father was uneasy about him; he respected his father-in-law, but it was clear that he resented him as well. A professor of Spanish literature and humanities for twenty-three years, he admired Artemio for all he had written and for his accomplishments as an editor and publishing entrepreneur. His evaluation of his writing, however, was not as generous. In my dad's eyes, Artemio Precioso wrote light fiction—superficial and subservient to popular and uncouth tastes. My father was not the only one to voice this opinion. Artemio had been typecast as a pornographer by people whose judgment on such things was suspect at best and ruinous at worst. Every now and then my father used these judgments against my mother when they argued. And my mother responded with her own righteous indignation in defense of her father. I remember the disputes—there were many of them in my family. When my mother would launch into her dramatic lamentations about how poorly her father was treated, my father would say, in his eloquently uppity Spanish, "Your father was nothing but a pornographer."

Today I think I know what all that was about. It had to do with the *relación sanguínea* (the blood relationship), something at the core of difficulties of their lives together. No denying that Paco had married his sister's daughter, a union not exactly made in heaven. The entire family saw it as a horribly bad idea, something my mom and dad would have to live with for their entire lives. That's why my mom was so defensive about her father's alleged pornography and it's why my dad was quick to point it out. He was perceived by Mercedes' family, especially her father, as someone in pursuit of something illegitimate. So my dad fought back as if to say "Who was he, a pornographer, to have questioned my motivations when I was courting you?" I found a revealing passage in my grandfather's memoir of his years in Parisian exile in which he defends his intimate friend the novelist, Blasco Ibáñez, against a *realista* (royalist) who called his writings "morally twisted and perverse." "I'm a realist in literature," asserts Artemio, because "to be a realist [meaning monarchist] in politics is equivalent to incest." His rhetorical use of the word "incest" in royal marriages hit me, because it reminded me of my mother's relationship to her husband-uncle.

There were many stories of Artemio's opposition to his daughter's marriage, notwithstanding that Paco was a handsome and serious student, a would-be diplomat and a man of ambition. I now remember one conversation in particular: she told me in all her theatricality that her father intercepted letters written to her from my dad, then her boyfriend. Artemio would crumple them up into a ball, she said, and throw them in her face. Mercedes would enact the scene as she formed a fist with the imagined letter in her hand, exclaiming as if she were a teenager, "But I love him, and he loves me back!" In her words, *me corresponde*—a heartfelt allusion to requited love in all its glory. My grandfather would reply with comments on the writing in my dad's letters, she said. Apparently, he had misspelled the word for selfish *egoísta* with an "h" *hegoísta*, something of an elementary mistake for a university student. But today I'm skeptical of that; my grandfather was fishing for errors. I can attest to the fact that my father wrote remarkably well in his books and his letters both in Spanish and English, although the English came later. What Artemio objected to, was the taboo of blood mixture. Understandably so. I've given much thought to this uncommon union, and I'm sure I would not like it if my daughter had wanted to marry her uncle, no matter the time or the culture. I remember my father telling me that if I had a relationship with a daughter of my mom's stepmother it would be okay. I suspect he told me this not as an encouragement but to relieve his trepidation at the reality of his own relationship.

Eventually Artemio gave in, although it must have been with grave reservations. He let my father know of his reluctant acceptance of the marital union. It seems they all resigned themselves to the fact. My dad always acknowledged my grandfather's importance and his steadfast actions in defense of democracy, free speech, and independent thinking despite having been diminished by him.

Mercedes' sentiments were equally ambivalent. She loved her father despite his absence, and she loved her soon-to-be husband, no matter the family disapproval at the time of their courtship and well after. In many ways she was engaged in an illicit love affair, not unlike the wistfully young love of her own mother and father when they were about the same age as Paco and Mercedes. Perhaps for that reason her love of Paco was exciting—forbidden fruit. I surmise that some of my mother's later problems stem from that passionate, innocent love for my father, a love that possibly left her without the affection of her own father. Artemio had to accept it eventually, but the marriage of the eldest daughter of the prominent writer to her own uncle was not something he wished to discuss in public. It was the early thirties, and the much-awaited fall of Artemio's nemesis, the dictator Miguel Primo de Rivera, along with the fall of the monarchy, the advent of the Second Republic, and the coming of the Civil War, were more than enough for him to worry about.

Chapter Four

Mercedes in the Revolution

"Grandpa threw down the newspaper and let out a curse." That's how Elena Fortún begins her tragic novel, *Celia en la revolución* (*Celia in the Revolution*), written soon after the Spanish Civil War, but not published until 1987 because the powers that be did not like the way she depicted the war, descriptions that most Spaniards, in the immediate years following the war, wanted to forget. Who can blame them? Virtually every Spanish person I know, no matter their political perspective, who has read about Celia in the Civil War has told me it was a difficult read despite its captivation and accessibility. As a professor of Spanish literature, I shared my readings and classroom experiences with my mother, and I suggested she read this novel. She never did as far as I know, probably due to her survivalist inclination to stay away from ugly realities. Her sister Marina did; she started reading this novel after I lent her my copy when I was living in Alicante on a sabbatical leave. She told me she got halfway through and could not continue because it was too painful.

Written for young adults, *Celia in the Revolution* is the last in a series of novels about a sassy teenager from an upper-middle-class family who asks too many questions about class differences, romance, and customs, and as a result, she gets herself in a lot of trouble. In virtually all the previous novels in the series she tries the patience of the adults, despite her charm, something like a Spanish *Anne of Green Gables*. But not as much when the "revolution" comes; here she is the epitome of responsibility and perseverance. Grandpa's act of throwing down the newspaper marks the beginning of her family travails, some horrific. One might compare *Celia in the Revolution* to many works written about Nazi Germany from a Jewish perspective. Spaniards were weary of the death and suffering that permeated just about all of Spanish life at that time. That Celia's grandpa was angry about the military uprising against a duly constituted Republic in 1936—an event that brought on the Spanish Civil War along with the beginning of the end of Celia's well-being—is something about which many Spaniards can say, "Yes, my grandpa reacted the same way."

For my mom, like Celia, things also changed drastically with the war, but she did not experience anything like Celia's woes. Celia was in her teens; my mom was in her twenties. Celia's family was relatively well-to-do, as was my mother's, but Mercedes had the added advantage of being the daughter of the civil governor of Toledo in 1934 and of Lugo from 1935 to 1936—although those fortunes would later turn into strikes against her and the family. Celia experienced hunger, and was an eyewitness to death and destruction, much of it involving her loved ones. While my mom experienced nothing as severe as Celia's hardships, that does not diminish the intensity of those years for that well-off girl from Hellín, both joyful and terrifying—mostly terrifying. War tends to wind the clock of Memory, but it also begs us to forget, which for Mercedes was the way she kept going.

Mercedes and Paco 1935

My mom and dad were married less than a year before the upheaval, the fulfillment of a promise of conjugal happiness deferred. Their courtship fascinates me. Mercedes told me that she first laid eyes on Paco in Hellín, but their relationship took hold in Paris. His family and friends called him Asis through his childhood, adolescence, and young adulthood. Asis is a name derived from St. Francis of Assisi. His presence at that time in that little town—today it is much bigger—has always been something of an enigma to me: Why was my father in Hellín, located in south central La Mancha if the Ugartes were from Vizcaya, a province of the Basque Country on the northern Atlantic coast? Given also that my grandfather Artemio married my dad's sister Marina, clearly there was something going on between the Ugartes and the Preciosos. To this day I'm not sure exactly what it was. The answer probably has to do with my paternal grandfather, Javier Ugarte Schultz, the brilliant (albeit crazy) mining engineer who had probably collaborated with Artemio's father in metallurgy enterprises and had brought his family to Hellín, where both my parents were born. Keep in mind that Javier the mining engineer was also my mom's grandfather (see the family tree). Thus, my dad, son of the engineer, and my mom, daughter of a rising young author who would eventually become governor, would have been in their teens when Cupid's arrow penetrated both hearts at once.

Around 1927 my pubescent mom took a look at Paco, whom she also called Asis, and she fell. She never told me she fainted or pretended to faint, or that she made a visible gesture as a girl her age might have done. I don't know if she even expressed to anyone that she had a crush on this young man; all she told me was that she really liked his looks. And when she told me about their first romantic encounter, she smiled from ear to ear. According to her, it was reciprocal. My dad had the same memory when he heard her talk about that first gaze; he too was taken by Merche—that's what her peers and family called her. They were just three years apart; my dad was the elder. It didn't matter that he was her uncle.

My mom told me they made contact in Paris the first year of Artemio's exile to France. My father went off to France too, but in his case, it was to start a career as a salesman. From Paris he went to the U.S. and Canada to work for Johnson & Johnson medical supplies and to take classes in business administration at Rutgers University. He had stopped off in Paris to visit the family. I still try to wrap my mind around the "blood relationship" and its consequences. Often, like you, reader, I have to stop and think about it. In any case, there was no doubt Paco and Merche experienced what some call maximum attraction.

An inner voice I don't listen to enough tells me that my father first looked at his niece with devilish desire walking by himself along a Parisian boulevard in the Etoile neighborhood, today named after Charles De Gaulle. He soon found out that Artemio had moved. Listen to the way a journalist from *El*

Heraldo de Madrid described the place where my mother's family lived in Paris—the Spanish press relentlessly interested in the lives of writers exiled from Primo de Rivera's regime:

> [Artemio Precioso Sr.] moved to a different neighborhood [in Paris]. From L'Etoile to Auteuil: from the Wagram Boulevard with all its cafés and theaters, to a splendidly peaceful part of town, Auteuil, a city in itself, with glorious fountains. Auteuil gives one the impression of a neighborhood filled with health spas, no grand cafés but lots of spacious parks. The Bolonia forest, avenues named after Mozart, Poussin, Henry Heine . . . Fusion of bourgeois and classical architecture associated with a sense of serenity and cleanliness, well-paved streets, all straight, leading to the Bolonia Park next to the race track (quoted in Francisco Linares' biography of Artemio Precioso).

The Parisian racetrack of the twenties and thirties is nothing like what we think of racetracks in the States. I remember my mom's eyes lighting up when I told her that Maurita, my then girlfriend and later wife and ex-wife, lived with her family in the backyard of Rockingham Park racetrack in Salem, New Hampshire. I did not know it then, but Mercedes surely thought back to her life in high-bourgeois Paris. She loved the image—reality be damned. When she saw Rockingham Park from Maurita's family's back yard, I'm sure she changed her mind.

A mental picture of a racetrack brought her back to the day she fell for Paco. The Preciosos lived in an upscale apartment building, even when they were having financial difficulties, a testimony to my grandfather's business acumen even in the face of pecuniary problems not of his making. My father was probably considered by the Preciosos as something of an outsider even though his sister Marina, now deceased, had been married to Artemio. I'm certain that when they saw my father they associated him with his notoriously crazy father, Javier, the engineer. My father was a man at once ambitious and melancholy; walking by himself gave him solace. As he headed toward the Bolonia Park, toward the Precioso's dwelling, he saw a young lady step out on the balcony to join her father, his face submerged in a newspaper. She took a look at the man walking toward their building and asked her father who he was. Artemio put down the newspaper and said that man was her uncle, but that comment had no effect. She had seen him before in Hellín, but now that he was staring at her from the street, something came over her.

For Paco it was different. Maybe he missed his deceased sister. Maybe he had a need for a tenderness that he did not get from his own family, a need for familial warmth given the difficult relationship with his father, known for his disdain for others and at times violence. In the family lore his father was said to have killed someone over a property disagreement—always in search of fortune, with little concern for his children. Asis grew up without the support, even disdain, of his dad, Javier Ugarte Shultz.

But my dad, I like to think, was also looking for the love of a woman; and Merche was open to romance. The proverbial arrow had hit its mark. Unbeknownst to them, it was the beginning of an attraction that would bring them both great joy and great conflict. I'm afraid the conflict outweighed the joy, but that might have to do with my own occasional predilection for darkness.

Full disclosure: I have no certainty that my mother and father met this way for the first time. But again, I'll follow my mom's lead and say, "Could be true and not have happened." If it didn't happen precisely this way, certainly the first encounter was, according to both of them, a moment of intense attraction. They both told me as much in their own way. They did indeed keep their infatuation going through correspondence. Both were lovesick. Would that one of them had kept those letters.

Ironically, all that love was followed by the Revolution. The violent political atmosphere in which my mom and dad lived during their courtship in the thirties is something many Spaniards of that time experienced. The king had abdicated, and the dictator had fled; shortly after, there were elections that brought on a new democratic government with no monarchy. This allowed my mom's dad to return from France with his family. Francisco too had returned from overseas business trips to begin his studies in the Law School of the Universidad Complutense of Madrid. Merche and her family had returned to life in Spain, taking up residence in Madrid close to the Retiro Park.

My grandfather's return from exile brought on hope despite the turmoil that followed. Certainly, Artemio was hopeful that a new Republic would allow for freedom, prosperity, and a more enlightened way of thinking among his fellow Spaniards. And Merche was equally hopeful, as was the majority of the Spanish population, with some all-too-notable exceptions. But I think my mom's hope had to do with that handsome young man to whom she was related and from whom she had received letters of affection.

While my dad was working toward his law degree just as the war began, their relationship grew, and the family became more and more resigned to it. My mom was deeply proud and enamored of Paco for his academic accomplishments and good looks. She remained so for many years, well after their move to the United States. The reciprocity of those feelings is less certain, yet looking at photos of my mom in the thirties and forties—both before and after their journey to the New World—it's likely Paco's yen for Mercedes persisted (until it didn't). In any case, Mercedes loved him completely, at times disconsolately. The tangible proof of his successes is the cap and gown that my mother kept for many years after his death, regardless of the advice to get rid of all his clothes. This advice was from me, I'm ashamed to admit. I concede that the good looks are a matter of taste, but she thought he was dashing in his cap and gown. Those graduation robes are now in my possession, and I have worn them to at least ten graduation ceremonies—I lost count—none of which were celebrations of my graduation, all were dedicated to my students.

That graduation gown has had a life of its own. After Paco and Mercedes had settled in at Dartmouth, commencement was a ceremony both attended nearly every year from 1947 to 1969, and my dad stood out. He looked like a cardinal; it was the basic graduation robe of the Law School at the Universidad Complutense, black with a hood the brightest of red. He had no need to feel daunted by all the Ivy Leaguers in his midst; his gown and his history were from a different place, a different time, and my mother with all her pride, indeed haughtiness, was the picture of a dark-haired Spanish beauty whose man had graduated from a place more sophisticated than Harvard. After all, he was an authentic European. Boston Brahmins be damned; being a European of good breeding is what Boston Brahmins aspired to be. Paco was well-liked and respected among the snotty Ivy League faculty. He made them look worldly, despite their provincialism.

I never bought a graduation gown of my own, never thought much of these pretentious rituals, until at one point I was thinking of my mom and dad in Madrid around 1935. This was the year embroidered in the inner lining of the gown; it was also the year of their wedding. Thinking of all that, I decided it was time to do as the fourth Catholic commandment says: honor your father and mother. I attended a good number of my students' graduations. I wish my mom could have seen them, but she was much too old to sit through those deadly ceremonies. I wish my dad could have seen them too—the regret of a man who still harbors fraught memories of his father.

These memories became those of "Revolutionary Spain," with all that my mom and dad told me about it, and all I read about the war that had defined the identity and being of my entire family, like so many Spanish citizens. After his exile in France, Artemio Precioso and family arrived at a fleeting moment of hope followed abruptly by social conflict, much having to do with the travails of her father, the civil governor of Toledo and then Lugo. Civil governors were appointed, not elected; Artemio Precioso was named governor of those two provinces because of his connections with the democratic Republican government. As a political/cultural figure, he was often in the news, often the object of criticism as he dealt with events and circumstances over which he had little control. My mom simply accepted both the pitfalls and privileges of having a father in the public eye. She was proud of him no doubt, and there is even less doubt that she enjoyed the prestige, the noblesse oblige and the status of being the governor's daughter. But the downside was all that conflict, often violent. My grandfather was not only Voltairian by his own description, he was a public man. The many people in Spain of that time who were neither freethinkers nor Voltairian thought my grandfather was causing all the ills of Spanish society. I see Mercedes walking along a street in Toledo or in Lugo as a young bride-to-be—there must have been some raised eyebrows, if not some open comments, like "There she is, *la hija del gobernador*, we'll see what happens to her when we get rid of them."

On the other side, when she and other *Republicanos* saw people on their way to mass, they would yell, "¡*Carcas a misa!*" (something like, "Go on to mass, you retrogrades!" or someone else might translate the word *carcas* as fascist creeps). The suggestion was that some people can't think for themselves. A comment like that—I'm sure it was common in her day—was not only unheard of after 1939, it could have landed you in jail. Those diehard nationalists, the ones that initiated the rebellion, Catholic to the core, got their way. Artemio Sr. would land in jail a few years later. His crime? To have been a politician with ties to the Republic.

The life of my mom's father in the years immediately following Mercedes' marriage is well known now, but we know precious little about how that tumultuous life effected his daughters. All I can do is imagine my mom as the daughter of the man whose advocacy of a free press, critical of a Catholic clergy that had deprived many Spaniards of their rights to worship freely and act with self-determination, would be the story of his public life. In 1934, newly appointed governor, he was eager to implement measures based on these principles. But things were not easy for him. The Republic was riddled by forces both to the left and right of his liberal ideals. The left had demanded that the traditional celebration of Corpus Christi, perhaps the most sacred of all religious holidays in all of Spain, especially in Toledo, be suspended: it was a matter not only of the separation of Church and State, but also of the tyrannical clutches of the Church over a defenseless population. And on the other side, the Church and the landowners whose property had come under scrutiny with the new government reacted vehemently against the suspension of the holiday. My grandfather did not succumb to the anticlerical demands. It was a strategic move on his part as well as one that came from his convictions. Strategically, suspending or abolishing the Corpus celebration would alienate a powerful right wing, eager to reinsert itself into power with a military coup. And ideologically, he genuinely thought people have a right to celebrate a religious holiday, especially one so dear to Toledo where he was a public official.

Fed up with the political clashes in his province, my grandfather was moved (or asked to be moved) to Lugo in 1935, where he was appointed again to a civil governorship and where his eldest daughter was married. I'm not sure if it was a public wedding. It's unlikely that my mom's family wanted to let people know that the oldest daughter of the writer-turned-politician was marrying her uncle. I don't know if anyone from my father's side attended the wedding. He must have had to secure a dispensation from the Church, given the *relación sanguínea* (blood relationship). I tried to find news reports on the nuptials, but couldn't, which was odd to me because it was the wedding of a daughter of a prominent man. I found a cursory announcement of the wedding in a newspaper from Lugo buried among other public notices, but precious little about the event. I sense that the governor had more important things on his mind in 1935. The political future of Spain was at stake in a general election that eventually led to the Civil War, and he was deeply involved. Unfortunately, I may never know the details of the wedding because I never asked my parents. I suspect Artemio Sr. pulled some strings and offered a sizable amount of *pesetas*.

From Lugo my mom moved to Madrid to be with Paco, and both would stay there until their departure for the greener democratic pastures of the United States. Mercedes' and Paco's life as newlyweds in the capital of a country filled with civil strife was at once perilous and exciting. As I think back to all my mother's trials leading to her mental instability, including paranoia, I can't help concluding that she had reason enough to be borderline insane. Celia (*Celia in the Revolution*) didn't go crazy, but as that novel ends, any reader senses the trauma the war caused, along with all the people who never recovered from that trauma—my mom was one of them. As a newlywed not exactly interested in politics, her first desire at this time must have been for her family's safety. And that desire was not always realizable. As some people say, "Just because you're paranoid doesn't mean they're not out to get you," and indeed *they*, both on the left and right, were out to get my mom's father.

My grandfather had come under fire in many ways. As governor he was in charge of overseeing the general elections in his province in 1936. These were the elections that solidified the democratic sovereignty of his side, the Popular Front, and the defeat of the right wing. Several months later the military coup that my grandfather and many others had tried to avoid erupted, and that meant that the Civil War was on. My mom and dad were relatively well-off because of my dad's position in the US embassy in Madrid. On the other hand, my grandfather is one of many who suffered. When Franco took power in 1939, he announced that "Anyone whose hands are clean, has no need to fear [imprisonment or execution]." But as any historian of the war will tell you, regardless of that person's political persuasion, Franco was being less than honest. Franco let loose a series of bloody reprisals, the trauma of which is still felt today. My grandfather barely escaped execution. He was sentenced to prison for what the Franco authorities called "supporting the rebellion"—ironic due to the fact that it was Franco who rebelled. Rebellion, for Franco and his ilk, was defined as treason against the Catholic national tradition, and that rebellion was foreign by definition, even though the supporters of the Republic, like my grandfather, could not be more Spanish. After time in prison, Artemio spent the last years of his life (1944 and 1945) under house arrest in a tiny town, Isso, just outside of Hellín. A year later my mom and dad set sail for the welcoming arms of post–World War II United States.

In my grandfather's unpublished *Autobiografía*, he describes his imprisonment and house arrest. But the question so few in the family asked is, What about his children? What about Mercedes? I am certain my mother was not even aware that her father was writing a memoir of his life while he was under house arrest—few in the family were. The truth, whatever we can rescue of it, is that my mom probably handled the political, physical, and emotional hardships of her father in the early forties by trying desperately and unsuccessfully to find out how he was doing, and later by trying, also unsuccessfully, to tell herself he was doing as well as could be expected.

But now that these things are in a remote past, I want to figure out what happened. In his autobiography, my grandfather talks about being in a five-by-five-meter cell with twenty prisoners in a Madrid detention center, and people on the street shouting insults at them through a tiny window. He also talks about two kinds of cruelty he witnessed as a political prisoner: prison authorities robbing the inmates of their possessions, and jail keepers taking pleasure in making the prisoners suffer physically. He talks about one man he does not name who was beaten to a pulp before being executed. "One last meal before you die?" the-soon-to be-dead prisoner was asked. "Not on your life," he replied.

My mom did not know of all this, at least not the details. Now that we are aware of the particulars, it's good she didn't. Of the general horror, of course she knew, as did my dad, but the specifics were not things she talked about. What my mom did know was that her father was in jail and that there was danger that he might be put to death. Information on his well-being trickled in to members of our family, particularly my aunt Marina, through rumors. My mom told me a little about this: that she brought him food when he was in the detention center on General Porlier Street in Madrid, that when he was moved to Hellín, her sister Marina told her about the firing squads and worried nightmarishly that their father had been another victim of the New Regime's reprisals, and that their father was in need of medical care and of virtually all necessities, including what was seen as not so necessary—a typewriter and paper. In his autobiography, my grandfather talks about a precious Remington typewriter that was provided to him due to the help of family members. Learning of this affected me a great deal. I saw a few of his letters written from prison—he was writing on paper with the imprimatur of the U.S. Embassy, which means that mom and dad must have tried successfully to make sure my grandfather got what he said he needed to stay alive: paper, the prime tool of his trade and his weapon of self-defense, perhaps as important as food and water. Believe it or not writing paper was not readily available at that time, much less a typewriter.

But Mercedes' accounts of the Civil War and its aftermath is not all pain and misery. In fact, the life of my mom and dad in the U.S. Embassy from 1935 to 1946 had its ups and downs. While things were good for them in comparison to most Spaniards, there was a terrible war going on, and some of their family members were in danger, either as participants or as dissidents living in Franco's territory. Madrid was under siege; Franco dropped bombs incessantly with the aid of Nazi Germany, especially after Nationalist troops had failed to take the city in the first year of the war. My dad told me that in that first year, like many able-bodied young men who supported the Republic, he answered a call to arms. He went to what would become the front line of battle on the outskirts of Madrid in the University area where he had studied, to join the antifascist struggle. He was met by a ragtag group of militiamen—he said they were anarchists—who told him to go home. They didn't trust him because he was wearing a tie, a sure signal that he sympathized with the other side, or so they thought. "*Puto burgués*" (Fucking bourgeois), they yelled at him, and "fascist son-of-a-bitch!"

My mother's reaction when her Paco told her he was going off to the Madrid front line of battle to defend the city was surely not joyous. I imagine that she feared not only for him, but for herself. It was the kind of wartime uncertainty that brought many people to insanity, or near insanity, because, after all, it was an insane situation. After yelling at him, I can see her desperately asking, "Why not stay put, Paco? You have a job at the U.S. Embassy. Here there are people who will protect you."

And ultimately, she was right. The U.S. Embassy in Spain under the Franklin Roosevelt administration of the thirties and forties treated Francisco Ugarte Cristobal well. Not only did both my parents say as much, it's in the historical record. Yet what I saw in that historical record of the U.S. Embassy is not only the dossier of a "native informant," a translator, whose service to the U.S. government the officials appreciated, it's the story of someone whose job performance was stellar, given the circumstances. Shortly after the war, the U.S. Secretary of State under FDR, Cordell Hull, wrote a letter to my dad thanking him for his service: "I wish to commend you for your excellent performance and for the courage and tact which you displayed under trying circumstances." Years later, in an evaluation form designed by the Embassy, Sydney B. Redecker, a career diplomat who at that time worked as an aid to then U.S. Ambassador to Spain, Claude G. Bowers, writes, "[Ugarte] is probably the most generally useful of all the Embassy's Spanish employees, and would be difficult to replace. During the Spanish Civil War, he performed especially meritorious service in caring for the Embassy and American interests in the absence of American personnel."

My dad told me he did all he could to protect citizens, Spanish and U.S., from Franco's wrath, and he was able to do this because of what he represented—a powerful U.S. government trying to decide what to do about Spain, indeed, what to do about a Europe on the verge of a catastrophic loss of democracy. In those years, all was up in the air. For my mother the uncertainty must have been much worse: her father had been sentenced to death and the whereabouts of her brother, an avowed communist who had fought against Franco, was unknown. He may have been dead for all she knew. She was pondering having children, but why? It was a difficult choice given not only the postwar strife, but the *relación sanguínea* (blood relation).

It is clear also in the documents related to Francisco Ugarte's employment in the Embassy in Madrid that he wanted to leave, and he wanted to do so from the very year the war ended. Several of his letters request a leave of absence from his job at the Embassy so that he could pursue employment in another country. In those letters, particularly one addressed to Bowers on

May 21, 1939, he explains his reasons: "My only ambition now is to go to the United States, or at least to leave this country. As you probably know, two of my brothers were killed fighting with the Republican Army; I have another brother in a French concentration camp. My father-in-law, Artemio Precioso, whom you probably recall was Civil Governor of Toledo in 1934, is now in prison. For these and other reasons it is very hard for me to continue in Spain. I [would] much rather work in the States for $20 a week than here for much more."

"For these and other reasons . . ." Clearly, he was fed up with the violence, wartime destruction, and an outcome not to his liking. It was his "only ambition" to go into exile, although he did not call it that—yes, I remember my father as an ambitious man, but that he didn't care if he'd have to work for less money is not convincing to me, knowing what I know of his preoccupation with family finances. But he wrote this letter at the very end of the Civil War; it shows a certain exasperation, even pathos, about all the death and destruction. His references to his brothers and father-in-law are compelling; he is at once sad and angry. Yet at the same time, the letter is a request to an employer, and its intention is to get a pass to another country.

The official record of the U.S. Embassy is only part of this. There is a personal story behind it, the story about his loved ones. I ponder how my mom was faring when she was a young and pretty bride of an up-and-coming Spanish diplomat. No doubt they talked about this. *"De este país nos tenemos que ir, Merche."* (We've got to get out of this country, Mercy). How Mercedes responded, I will never know; she never told me. I surmise that as a relatively young woman, she felt her place was next to her husband in all circumstances, especially in the aftermath of a war.

That's the way it was not only in Spain, but virtually throughout the world in the mid-twentieth century. It's only after the fact, with all that we have explored and learned regarding women's agency—and I am just one person in the collective "we"—that *we* think of how it was for women. "Supposing Truth is a woman—what then?" This is what Nietzsche asks in his first sentence to his famous work, *Beyond Good and Evil*. His sardonic style notwithstanding, it's an excellent question, and if we ask it at a time of social strife, it gives more than a few of us pause.

There are lots of Spanish women who wrote about and talked about that war, and to generalize about them has its drawbacks. Still, the kinds of gritty, multifaceted female perspectives of the Spanish Civil War, like the one shown in *Celia in the Revolution* by Elena Fortún and lots of others, such as the novel by Mercè Rodoreda, *La Plaça del Diamant*, translated by David Rosenthal as *Time of the Doves*, or Clara Campoamor's *La revolución española vista por una republicana* (*The Spanish Revolution as Seen by a Republican Woman*) add unexpected, nuanced details to the perspectives offered by men. Noteworthy also are the many texts written by non-Spanish women about the Spanish Civil War, like those of Martha Gellhorn in her stirring journalistic accounts of Spain at war and Josephine Herbst in *The Starched Blue Sky of Spain*. And that first one is of special interest to me because my mom, the wife of the guy the U.S. diplomatic corps left in charge of the Embassy, came into contact with famous people like Martha Gellhorn and Ernest Hemingway. Hemingway was interested in who was winning the war, while his then bride-to-be was mostly concerned for the personal lives of everyday Spaniards, especially children, regardless of political persuasion.

During the war, Gellhorn and Hemingway stayed in the Hotel Florida on the Callao Plaza in the center of Madrid. The hotel was popular among the many foreign war correspondents and writers who wanted to be in the thick of things, and the Gellhorn-Hemingway couple was among the most prominent. In Hemingway's famous propaganda film in favor of the Republic, *The Spanish Earth*, there are images of this grand hotel built in 1924 at the heyday of all the new shops and cafés along the Gran Vía Avenue, monuments to Spanish entrance into the capitalist world. After their marriage, mom and dad took walks along that boulevard, and my mom loved it. The liveliness, the modernity—not to mention that she was a newlywed married to a rising diplomat—awakened her sensations. But with the war her sensations changed—from excitement to fear. It was only in the visits to the Embassy by all these prominent people that she saw what looked to her like a few passing benefits of the war. From what Mercedes told me about those days, I surmise she was familiar with the goings-on at the Embassy as the wife of the dashing young Spaniard in charge who spoke English oh so elegantly and as the daughter of a prominent writer-politician. I ask myself today if my mom and dad ever ventured over to the Hotel Florida to meet with these public figures—it's more likely that they came to see my father in his office at the Embassy. But the aura of the Hotel Florida was no less a part of their lives at that time. Today the huge lot where the Hotel Florida once stood is—what else—the Corte Inglés, something like the Macy's of Spain, another landmark of Spain's entrance into the world market.

Many years later I attended a conference dedicated to literature of the Spanish Civil War, and there I met Martha Gellhorn, who was in her eighties. She had agreed to participate in the conference under the stipulation that she not be asked to talk about Hemingway. But in the culminating public dialogue of the conference between her and the Spanish novelist, Juan Benet, in which the latter said he thought that *For Whom the Bell Tolls* was a superficial novel, she smiled and nodded in agreement. That was in the mid-nineties; at the time I did not think I'd be writing about my mother's life during the Spanish war, and, the sad truth be told, neither my mom nor my dad told me about Martha Gellhorn's presence in Madrid when they were at the Embassy. My dad did talk about Hemingway and seemed to share Benet's and Gellhorn's opinion that the author's bell was tolling a bit too loudly—lots of stereotypes and an overblown rendition of those poor international communists having to put up with Spanish indiscipline. Gellhorn could have told him as well that his portrayal of women in the novel is not credible. *For Whom the Bell Tolls* is about a graduate teaching assistant who goes to Spain to lend his technological services to the Spanish communists who are about to blow up a bridge. There he meets María—such an original name—and of course falls in love with the "pretty [leftist] señorita" whose political cadre is made up of illiterate peasants. The guy we're rooting for—the smart one, of course—is the student from Montana, Robert Jordan. The dialogue is filled with the second-person singular "thou" to simulate the Spanish formal *usted*, and fake archaic English that's supposed to be Spanish. My dad never put it in those words, but I remember him saying something like, "*Miguel, esa novela se equivoca.*" (Miguel, that novel gets it wrong). I'm probably being unfair—undoubtedly Hemingway wrote great novels and stories—but the one about the Spanish Civil War was not one of them.

After I came back from that conference, I told my mom I had met Martha Gellhorn (if only briefly), and Mercedes let me know that she too had met her. I jumped at the information and began to ask questions. What she remembered was that Gellhorn was *simpática* (friendly), gentle, and pretty; also, that she was Hemingway's translator. She spoke Spanish much better than he. My mom thought that if it weren't for Gellhorn, Hemingway would not have gotten the information about the war he was looking for as a writer-journalist. My dad, on the other hand, in keeping with the prevalent view of women as appendages of their husbands, did not consider including Hemingway's companion (if he remembered her) in his descriptions of his experiences of the war.

Hemingway wasn't the only one to have visited the Embassy under my dad's watch. Joe Kennedy stopped by too. He was the eldest of the Kennedy sons, who, according to his father, was first in line to become president of the U.S. This visit too became part of the Ugarte family lore. I remember that my mom smiled eagerly and warmly when she told listeners—there were many of them—that Joseph Kennedy danced with her at a reception at the Embassy. That coy glint in her eye and her acute sense of the theatrical led my father to call her Sarah Bernhardt (the famous actress of the twenties) for the way she captured people's interest. What would become one of my mom's most endearing and curious traits—her naughty allusions to illicit romance—was in full view when she described JFK's older brother (then in his twenties): "Oh verry [rolled r's] hansom, *muy muy guapo*, young, blond." Yes, he was young, five years younger than my dad, and that made him even more desirable to her. There are several photos of my dad posing with Joseph Jr. in front of the U.S. Embassy. My mom's impression of the young man on his way to the presidency bears itself out. Like virtually all the Kennedys, he was a good looker with his eyes wide open to possibilities with women, even the ones older than he. My father, to his credit, did not bear out the cliché of the jealous Spaniard, in fact I suspect he might have been happy to see that young Joseph enjoyed being the object of attraction to his pretty wife. Indeed, a little flirtation may have been just what they all needed in such a precarious political/military situation. There is a photo of my dad sitting with Joseph Kennedy Jr. on the front steps of the U.S. Embassy in Madrid, circa 1936 or 1937. Joe Kennedy Jr. and what he may have been referred to "Our Man In Madrid," Francisco Ugarte. Although I do not own a copy, I found it shown on the International Center of Photography website.

Yes, that political/military situation was precarious. At the time of the Kennedy visit to Madrid, there was still hope that Franco's forces would be defeated, but later, things fell apart, both in Spain, and in my family. First there were the bombs and shells. After the Nationalists failed to take Madrid in the early months of the war, the *Generalísimo* strategized a bombing campaign with the help of Nazi Germany. The fact that Franco had solicited and received support from the Number One Teutonic Tyrant of Europe made those bombs devastating not only in a physical sense, but in a political sense as well, especially to the many *Madrileños* who called themselves antifascists. Yet all the citizens of Madrid, no matter their political persuasion, were subjected to these bombs. Among countless Spaniards who were traumatized by the blood and destruction of those years was my mom. Like one of Elena Fortún's wartime characters, my mother spoke often about having to rush into bomb shelters with her husband and other neighbors, in refuge from Franco's bombs and artillery attacks. After she moved to the States, her rants about those years were often incoherent because she never mastered English, and many listeners did not speak Spanish. She didn't know the word for shell or mortar, so as she talked about the terror, she would almost always use the Spanish word *obús* (artillery shell). And she blurted out that word several times, opening her eyes wide and emphasizing that last syllable, always putting special stress on that "boo," as in boom. But it was her eyes and her dramatics that made her listeners sympathize—I among them. It was a story I heard often, from the time I could barely figure out what had happened to my parents in the thirties.

For me, *obus* became the sound of what my mother and father had lived, despite the fact that in comparison with many Spaniards, things were going relatively well for them. All this makes me remember the years when I too called myself a revolutionary in support of the Black Power movement and a protester opposed to the war in Vietnam. My mother was not like me, she was not deeply involved in politics. She was, however, a woman who knew about the devastation of war. Mercedes lived through a war and felt the wounds it had caused in her throughout her life. I was no eye-witness; in my twenties I saw the Vietnam war on TV; Mercedes saw it on TV too, but she had something to compare it with....

Chapter Five

Mercedes after the Revolution

"It was the spring of hope, it was the winter of despair . . . We were all going direct to Heaven, we were all going direct the other way." That's what Charles Dickens says about the London of his day. There was hope for Mercedes and Paco in Madrid at war's end, because they thought that perhaps they might begin a new life elsewhere, and Paco's position in the U.S. Embassy might make that hope a reality. More important was that they were thinking about having a child as a manifestation of that hope, much against the advice of the family.

But we needn't forget, and they never forgot, that Spain after Franco's victory was in a cruel winter of despair, and Madrid was one of many cities in which the ruins of war were palpable. They lived close to the Retiro Park, which was relatively unscathed, but in many other parts of the city there were buildings and entire streets in shambles. While countless Spaniards did not know where their loved ones were, Paco learned of the casualties of his two brothers. My mother knew that both Artemios were not well; the elder was in prison, and the whereabouts of the younger one was unknown. Mercedes' hope for a better future was no doubt tempered by her uncertainty about the safety of her father and brother. In the case of Artemio Jr., he was something like a soldier missing in action, and to some, being the loved one of an MIA is worse than being a widow or a sibling of a wartime corpse.

We learned years later that Artemio Jr. and a group of Republican soldiers had managed to commandeer a plane that landed them in Oran (Algeria), an area still resisting the Nazi-dominated government of France. Since they didn't know how to fly a plane, they landed by the skin of their teeth in a wheat field with peasants moving toward the wreckage. As soon as they hit ground in quasi-miraculous safety, they were carted off to a concentration camp. Months later, through a politically opportunistic agreement, he and several of his communist fellow prisoners were given the opportunity to move to the Soviet Union, and there he stayed and raised a family. He was not alone—there were some two thousand Spaniards who went into exile in the Soviet Union after the Civil War. Mercedes' brother did all he could to be of service to the cause of pro-Russian antifascism, including training Soviet troops in their war against Germany. He became disenchanted with the Russian regime, came back to Spain in the 1960s, turned into an environmental activist, and made a life for himself and his children—not without difficulty in his first years of arrival back in Spain.

But my mother knew nothing of this until later; none of the Precioso family members did. I recall, as in a dream, the day my mom told me about the moment she and Paco received a telegram with the news that her brother Artemio was alive and well. I don't know the number of tears my mom shed for her brother or for her father in the early years just after the Francoists took power. Neither am I certain how old I was when she told me about them, just that I was a boy. I remember my mom sobbed, and that confused me not knowing at that moment the difference between weeping out of pain or emotional stress. But as her life went on, she tried to forget about her brother's life during and immediately after the war. I was too young to truly understand all the circumstances; today I link that surreal intentional forgetfulness was my mom's way of coping with her various traumas.

The whereabouts of Mercedes' father in the forties, unlike those of her brother, were well known—he was in Franco's prisons. At the very moment of the end of the civil war, he was arrested, as were many other Spaniards who had supported the Republic—that is, they had committed the crime of what the Regime called "fomenting the rebellion." This "crime" is pathetically ironic: those who rebelled against a democratically elected government accused the supporters of that government of having rebelled against the rebellion. What? In other words, the true insurgents led by Franco defined themselves falsely as the ones in (true) power in 1936. Both my mom and dad knew that the crime was among the most contradictory and hypocritical that Franco and his cronies had conjured up.

Just prior to the end of the war, my grandfather had moved back to Hellín, tired of playing an active role in the defense of the Republic. The government gave him an insignificant job in charge of the courthouse where, in his own words, "There was nothing to do." But almost immediately after the fall of the Republic he was arrested, tried, and sentenced to twelve years and a day. This sentence was later reduced to seven years. His accusers first sought the death penalty, later accusing him of another crime of being a Freemason. It was a trumped-up charge, yet not unique among the thousands who were accused of treason for opposing the Franco insurgency. There were Masons in Spain since the eighteenth century, and they were active in Spanish political and cultural life as people who presented an alternative to conservative nationalistic Catholicism. Throughout the twentieth century, they provoked the ire of the Catholic Church as well as that of Francoist generals. Because of Masonic secretiveness, there was a conspiracy theory perpetrated by the right wing in Spain that Masonry was the prime force—a godless one—in the destruction of Catholic Spain. After several years of investigation of his case by the newly ruling judicial authorities, he was found not guilty, although the charge of "rebelling against the Francoist state" was upheld.

Looking into the civil-war and post–civil-war archives, I learned that Artemio Sr. was transferred several times during his prison sentence. At war's end, he spent time in Madrid's General Porlier detention center, where my mom and dad had occasional contact with him, since they were also living in Madrid. Along with many relatives of loved ones in Spanish prisons of the forties, my mother told me she brought food to the jail for her father. From the Porlier jail, Artemio Sr. was sent to the newly established prison in Puerto Santa María at the very southern tip of Spain, where his case was revisited and his sentence reduced to house arrest in a village, Isso, next to Hellín. Isso is where he spent the last two years of his life, and it was the most likely place for him to have written his *Autobiografía*.

My mom and dad worried a great deal about Artemio Sr. while he was detained. I'm not sure when my mother's uncanny ability to forget unpleasant occurrences out of a survival instinct came into play, but surely her worries about her incarcerated father arose later in her life. Like many Spaniards she was desperate. There were firing squads all over Spain whose victims were people who had supported the Republic. There was still a possibility that he could be among those victims. I ask myself today how my mom would have reacted if, sixty years after all this turmoil, I had made her aware of Artemio Sr.'s description of his time in prison. While she must have known the larger circumstances of his incarceration—the places, the time spent, culminating in his house arrest and death in 1945—she did not know the details. Few people did. With the exception of my uncle, who sought to learn what happened to his father when he returned to Spain from the Soviet Bloc. We knew little of my grandfather's life in prison. We didn't know that when he was transferred from Madrid to Puerto Santa María, over four hundred miles away, and that he was forced to tread at least part of the way by foot, despite the fact that he was sick and overweight. I can only imagine the journey, first in a ramshackle railway car with other prisoners, then off the train and proceeding on foot since much of the rail system had been destroyed. My mom's dad was one of many who were seen at that time chained together walking through the towns and countryside of Spain only to arrive—if they got there without dying—at another prison. Some of the residents of the towns they trudged through, upon seeing them, would spit or curse at them as a gesture of revenge or, just as likely, as a way to show the authorities that they were on the right side.

One of Spain's premiere novelists, Manuel Rivas, depicts the historical memory of the Spanish Civil War some sixty years after it all happened in a story adapted to film, *La lengua de las mariposas* (*Butterfly's Tongue*). It's about a school teacher, Don Gregorio, in a village in Galicia just as the Civil War was about to break. The teacher has a special relationship with a timid boy, Moncho, whose intellectual and moral curiosity is stimulated by his teacher. He tells of a butterfly's tongue, three times the length of the butterfly, the instrument of pollination. Don Gregorio tells the boy not only of the power of scientific observation, but also of the tremendous force of nature, manifested in *espiritrompa*, the scientific term for the tongue of the butterfly. Don Gregorio is an empiricist and a freethinker, and his thoughts are dangerous in the atmosphere of an entire society about to be seized by political and intellectual subjugation. The new military authorities arrest him toward the end of the film for supposed criticism of Catholic belief, and escort him with other political prisoners to the truck that will take him to prison. The villagers, including Moncho's family, shout insults at the beloved teacher: "Red." "Atheist." "Son of a bitch." "Satan." In the culminating images, Moncho at first seems reluctant to call Don Gregorio a good-for-nothing anti-Christ, but in the end, he chimes in with the rest of the crowd. "Atheist, Red," he repeats. His final insult to his teacher, however, is in code: *"Espiritrompa!"* he cries, as if it were the worst trait a human being could have—an indication to spectators that Don Gregorio's lessons are still in the mind of his student despite the circumstances. From now on, however, Moncho will have to speak in code.

Many years later I watched the movie with my mother at Ragtag Cinema in Columbia, Missouri. I thought it would remind her of her father's travails after the war, but she sat through the film expressionless as I sobbed. While my association of Don Gregorio with my grandfather was something of a stretch, it was not completely implausible. While both author and filmmaker wanted to kindle the memory of an audience thirsting for the "other version" of the events before, during, and after the war, it is difficult to think back today that the loved ones of another generation were paraded through villages as pariahs, misfits, unrepentant criminals being punished for their supposed misdeeds. *"Yo no he hecho nada"* (I have done nothing wrong) is something of a refrain in the many artistic works about the ravages of war endured by supporters of the Republic. My grandfather had done nothing wrong.

While Artemio Sr.'s death sentence was commuted, perhaps the worst punishment of all was the public humiliation—a man suddenly a pariah among writers, friends, and journalists who had respected him and now either shunned him or pretended not to know him. All told, the seven years turned out to be a death sentence after all: arrested in 1940, dead in 1945 at age fifty-four, indirectly or directly due to the conditions of life in Franco's prisons. All this was eating away at Mercedes, even though (unlike her sister Marina, who still lived in Hellín) she wasn't privy to the daily details of her father's house arrest in Isso. She was living in Madrid with Paco. As time went by, she pushed the memory of her father out of her mind. It was yet another strategy of survival: the truth is too painful, so why not pretend it didn't happen, or say, "Could be true and not have happened."

My mom's composure as she watched *Butterfly's Tongue* was in some ways admirable, yet it bothered me. I secretly wanted her to break down in desperate grief so that I could wallow in the cathartic moment. But no. Straight-faced and under control, she just stared at the screen. Although I tried not to show it, I sobbed when I saw Moncho's face as he mimicked the villagers' hatred of the teacher and accompanied the insults with a word he learned from his teacher. As we left the theater, I remember an awkward conversation with a local politician who was anxious to learn of the historical context of the film and expected me to explain professorially what the film was referring to as I was guiding my mom to the exit. I told him, "you'll just have to ask my mother," as we walked away. Bad move on my part; it was a good question and asked in all sincerity.

Post–Civil War Spain, many say, was worse than the war itself: hunger, infirmity, and perhaps just as unbearable, not knowing if someone on the winning side of the war would denounce you for your political allegiance. But there were good times too, many moments of pleasure, smiles, and laughter. I wasn't around then, but I've witnessed something like that in family photos taken in the forties. At one of those moments my brother was born: Jorge was the first born of Paco and Mercedes. It was in the midst of those postwar years that Paco and Mercedes Ugarte had a child, and his name was Jorge or George, like the first president of the United States—a tribute to democracy itself. It was July 3, 1943—a perfect date for a birth in a family of admirers of U.S. politics and society. George would do well far away from the *Escombros de la guerra* (debris of the war), as my dad often described to those he met in the U.S. who asked him about Spain. In contrast to many Spaniards, the couple had something bright looming ahead. Still, that future was no less precarious, as my father's move to another continent was by no means certain. Reality asserted to them that the side they had supported had lost a civil war, and the ill effects of that defeat might very well persist regardless of their desires to leave. What would happen? More uncertain still was the health of the child they'd decided to have despite the warnings of the family. After years of disapproval, the family had finally accepted the marriage with the understanding that they not have children.

"Your children will be monsters," was a warning my mom had gotten from several family members. It was a prohibition of the kind that parents give their child when they say, "Don't go near that house," the place of taboo. But not have children? I heard my father say many times that he felt sorry for a couple with no children; my mother heard him, and I'm certain she felt the same way despite the family's warning. My father thought he had a great birth-control method in *coitus interruptus*. He told me as a teenager that he himself had used this form of "withdrawal."

Years later, I remember asking my Mom about *coitus interruptus*, and she looked at me as if I were speaking to her from a different planet. I think she was feigning lack of knowledge, because she loved talking about what led to it, courtship, love at first sight, physical attraction, as in hair color, height, long legs, curves, lips, voice cadence, hands, and a long etcetera. But the "act," hands touching certain body parts, arousal, climax, that was never part of the discussion, at least not with me.

Coitus interruptus notwithstanding, Jorgito came along in the atmosphere that was the postwar wasteland of the forties. The fact was that Jorgito was perfect: ten fingers, two legs and arms, and a little fuzzy black hair on top of a nearly bald head. For my mother, he was a manifestation of the fundamental goodness of herself and her family, amidst the literal and figurative darkness—power outages were commonplace, and misery was all around. There are photos of my older brother taken from the time he was in my mom's womb, 1943, to 1946 (the year they set sail for the New World), all revealing that air, however tenuous, of happiness and optimism. Of course, that's what the family album is supposed to emanate. Here is Jorgito when he was baptized. My father's eyes are fixed on him as my mother holds him over the baptismal font. And here he is in his crib, and in another he sits up in front of a window; scrolled on the photo with what seems to me my mother's writing is "George Madrid." In another he is standing outside in a beautifully tailored coat that looks like a dress with a bicycle in the background. And there is my dad's writing, "*Jorge a los 14 meses* (at fourteen months)—1944." And that Jorge-George would accompany them on their voyage out of Spain and into a New World.

Their happiness is visible in our family album: photos taken in the Retiro Park, a short walk from their comfortable apartment. I recognize some of the spots—how little things have changed amidst this new Spain of today. But not all are in Madrid; there is one of Jorge splashing on the shore of a beach. The writing—I see my mom's letters—says "Santa Pola." I recall my mother telling me she used to vacation in Alicante before the war. But I have no idea how they got to Santa Pola—on the Mediterranean some four hundred kilometers southeast of Madrid—since the trains were barely operating, and you needed special governmental permission to travel from one province to another. Then again, to Francisco Ugarte, the man left in charge of the U.S. Embassy, perhaps that permission was not a problem.

As I look at other images of my mom's life before both George and I were born, I'm struck by how happy and beautiful it all looks in the immediate aftermath of the war. Yes, the best of times and the worst. There she is in Estoril, Portugal, in 1941. What were my parents doing in Portugal? She is standing on a rock in the middle of ocean water a few steps from the beach where the photographer (surely my father) snaps the shot. She has a bow in her hair, she smiles. And there she is in another picture sitting on a bench with my father with the *Río Tajo* (Tagus River) in the background the same year, probably the same trip. Memory, help me put this together, because you or someone or something has blurred my recollection of what my mother said about these photos well after my dad died. I remember she looked at them with me when I was in my twenties, and she uttered, "*Ah, Estoril.*" But she didn't fill me in on the details, or if she did, I don't remember them. So, it's up to me to fill in the blanks and repeat, "Could be true and not have happened."

At least two years had passed since the end of the war, and my father was still in charge of the Embassy. Perhaps he went to Portugal on an official visit and decided to take along his pretty and charming wife. And there they are the same year in Górliz, about thirty kilometers from Bilbao in the Bay of Biscay. A handsome couple—he thirty-one, she twenty-eight—in their bathing suits, fine figures, both of them smiling, proud of themselves, of their looks, of their situation. In another they are among some rocks, again in their 1940s swimsuits. He stands erect, smiling at some distant object (not at the camera) while she waves her right arm behind him, looking directly at the photographer. Who was taking the picture? I didn't even ask. And there is my dad in a small fishing boat about half a mile from shore. And there they are on the top of Archanda, the little mountain that skirts Bilbao just above the Nervión River, today known as the body of water flowing by the Guggenheim. In this photo they are dressed elegantly. He wears a sport coat and tie, dark slacks, and the serious expression of a man of some importance; she is demure as she locks her left arm in his, wearing a stunningly white jacket and dress, the wife of a man of some importance. And there they are again back in Madrid.

Here in another photo it's 1943 in what looks like the Retiro Park. She is very pregnant with George, wearing a full-length dress and the expression of a happily expectant mother standing next to her man. I'm looking at pictures of Paco, Mercedes, and their baby with landscapes in the background of the higher elevations outside Madrid. In all of them, everyone is smiling; it's all good. My mom and dad seemed determined to affirm not only that the family had been wrong about not having children, but also that life would continue *a pesar de* (in spite of) all the postwar misery. And this first child, the thing living in her womb: how would it come out?

Of course, these fading images don't tell the whole story. The smile on my mom's face when she was pregnant with Jorgito, the child everyone told her not to have, belies what she must have felt. Pictures might get somethings right, but they tend to lie. So here I am trying to figure all this out. Why did I not ask more questions about her lived experiences until I myself was approaching the next phase of my life—I'll call it post-middle age. As I pondered, I read a plethora of material on historical memory, not only Spain's, but that of other areas as well.

Art Spiegelman's *Maus* is one of them, a wrenching graphic novel about a son's inquiry into his father's experience of the Holocaust, a memoir that my daughter, Maura, suggested I look at again when I told her I was writing about her grandmother. Clearly, as in the rest of Europe of the forties, some people had more difficulties than others. My mom and dad, the Preciosos and the Ugartes, were in a tropical paradise compared to the family of Art Spiegelman. But they had it rough in their own way. Looking beyond the objective history toward the two people who raised me in relative comfort, I see a glaring contradiction. True, they were well-off, protected by the benefits of the U.S. Embassy, while the majority of their countrymen and women were in want.

Yes, they were faring better than most, but there's no reason to feel guilty about it. If they had turned to the Franco regime for economic and social betterment, if they had hosted parties for the high-ranking Francoist military personnel to further what became a cozy Cold War alliance in the forties and fifties between the U.S. and Spain, if my dad had denied that Artemio Precioso was not his father-in-law, or worst of all, if, upon his arrival in the U.S., he had turned into—as many European immigrants did—a raving anticommunist supporter of the McCarthy crusade, if any of those transformations had taken shape, this memoir would have taken another turn. My life would have taken another turn. But the reality is in the record; the anamnesis shows it in my mom's words, "Fascists we very sure weren't," and I might add never were. In fact, my mom and dad both told me that Paco, as the man in charge of the Embassy, did all he could (which was unfortunately not enough) to try to persuade the Franco authorities to ease up on the persecution of Republicans, even those Americans trapped in Spain during and after the war. This is one of the few issues on which Mercedes and Paco agreed. Yes, it was the number one reason for leaving dictatorial Spain.

Stories of wartime hardships of those days—not just in Spain, but in all of Europe in the thirties and forties—share certain tropes, often an attempt to reckon with past wrongs, an urge to set the record straight. Actually, my grandfather's tone in his autobiography is tame, understated, by comparison to that of *Maus*. But *Maus*'s main feature, the one that provided the impetus of the entire story, is close to the motivation of the story I'm writing now about my mom. It's a loved one's quest to find out what happened in all the gory, terrifying, lively, absurd details. Why? Not as much to gain a political point or to get even, as to let us all know the details of what happened, a reckoning, a catharsis, a conversation with the therapist. Sometimes these war stories tell just how much your family members suffered, as if we were all competing for degrees of victimhood, but that's not *Maus*'s motivation, and it's not mine.

Readers, take a look at a thought-provoking assessment of historical memory by David Rieff: *In Praise of Forgetting*. Rieff, whose mom was Susan Sontag, questions compellingly that oft-quoted statement that has now become a cliché, "Those who do not remember their past are condemned to repeat it." Sometimes, says Rieff, according to the circumstances, it's best to forget, or at least let it lie for a while. My mom was very good at that. Although for her, the ghost of the past would often come back to haunt, to destroy, seek revenge. Maybe we should welcome that ghost for what she is, an eerie phantasmagorical reminder of what went on. However, Rieff seems to suggest that in the long run, maybe if we treat the ghost right, that is, if we welcome her into our house, seek to understand her, if we look at the past as a series of events that might provide insights into human behavior in all its complexity, we might be the better for it. What we need to forget is revenge. It's not as much a matter of forgetting, as understanding. Yes, my mom was good at forgetting, but at the same time, she let the ghost into the house. I think maybe the ghost was Mercedes herself.

Left to right: Marina (sister), Artemio Jr., Mercedes.
circa 1918

Standing: Artemio Sr.
Seated (left to right): Mercedes, Artemio Jr., Marina
circa 1925

Left to Right: Mercedes, Artemio Jr., Marina.
Hendaye, France; circa 1934

Left to right: Marina, Artemio Sr., Mercedes, possibly Soledad, Mamá Amelia.
Tagus River, Toledo, Spain; circa 1934

Mercedes
Toledo 1934

Mercedes
Hellin 1935

Honeymoon 1935

Mercedes.
Galicia (Spain); circa 1935

Mercedes and Paco (Francisco)
1937

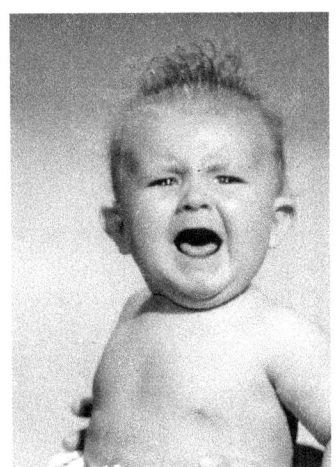
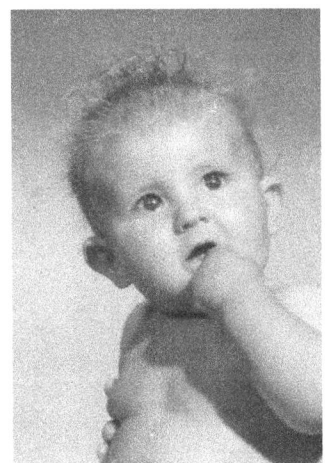

Jorge age eight months
1944

Mercedes with Jorjito
age fourteen months
Madrid, 1944

Part III

Chapter Six

Setting Sail for Life in New England

It was time to leave Spain. After her first son, George, was born, after the death of her father, after she had gotten news that her brother was alive and safe, after her husband decided he did not want to stay in Franco's Spain considering the death of his two brothers, after all her family had endured (along with so many Spaniards), after all that, she had stopped counting the tears she had shed. Mercedes was ready for a new life in a new continent with her Paco. She was at once excited and uneasy.

It was the end of World War II and there was now virtual certainty that Franco would remain in power regardless of the allied victory. The departure, the break with the *madre patria* (mother fatherland) was my dad's decision. My mom went along not just to be with her husband, but also because she too was yearning for a new situation. Although the story they told about their departure to friends, to their children, and to themselves was a tale of longing for something new, there was another version of that story that, with time, I became aware of.

But there was something else looming for Mercedes. If they were going to set sail, she would have to learn a new language, and it would have to be more than uttering the name of her son in English. I remember her voice as she said "George." She would say it with much flare, extending the "g" sound and rolling the "r" as her eyes would light up. I think she preferred her two sons' names in English, but she almost always called us Jorge and Miguel. While speaking the language of George Washington was always a major difficulty for my mom, my father had no problem. He was a fluent speaker of English at an early age due to a three-year stay in the U.S. and Canada while working toward a business degree, and his linguistic abilities were a valuable asset.

His older brother, Javier Ugarte Cristóbal, the firstborn of the crazy engineer and his wife, Micaela, was not only an English speaker, he was an avowed Anglophile. Fortunately, he had made it through the war without having to participate in it. It didn't hurt that he had supported the Nationalists by joining the fascist youth (JONS), a fact not included in my dad's letter to the ambassador. My uncle Javier loved Great Britain, the formality of its people, the courtesy, the refinement—at least among the class in which he circulated. He was a Basque gentleman in every sense. My father admired his older brother a great deal, not for his politics, which were secondary in his life, but for his hard work, business acumen, and good sense. Remember that he was also my mom's uncle, avuncular, a man the family could rely on. My mom spoke well of Tío Javier and the elegant Catalan woman he married, Elvirita.

That he was my dad's favorite brother, and that he had had experience in other countries endeared him to Mercedes. Tío Javier and Tía Elvirita were always held in high esteem by my parents, politics aside. She chose to consider Javier her elderly uncle rather than her brother-in-law; he was eighteen years her senior and a good, responsible man. I am certain that his Anglophilia rubbed off on my father, who considered Javier something of a surrogate parent, since Javier Sr. (my paternal grandfather, Ugarte Schultz, the engineer) suffered from what would probably be considered today schizophrenia.

My dad told me that one night while having a family dinner Javier, my father's dad, took out his false teeth and yelled at everyone while the false teeth clicking up and down in his hand. To think that this was my mother's grandfather—remember that Paco was her uncle too—is baffling, but it also might very well be a genetic trait explaining my mom's strange behavior later on. Ugarte Schultz was extravagant, cruel, and abusive, known for violence toward my grandmother Micaela. He abandoned the family several times, thus leaving the fatherly parental duties to my dad's brother Javier. My dad loved his older brother for this and for his worldliness, his respect for all things English, a love that was shared by my mom as well, even though on the Precioso side, there was more cultural appreciation for things French than British.

While my dad showed off his linguistic prowess as often as he could, traveling to the U.S. and Canada working for various companies before his definitive departure from Spain, my mom's new task was to learn to speak an unfamiliar tongue, to make sounds she was not used to making. Paco helped her, but it was difficult, and her success not always audible. Her relationship with the English language was multifaceted. Years later as a child I was embarrassed, typical of many children of recent immigrants. But as the years went by, that changed; I was not as much embarrassed as eager to correct, an eagerness that had little or no effect, because, the more I encouraged her to pronounce things with an insipid American accent, the more Spanish she sounded, even though she was under the impression that her English was nearly perfect. Also, my mom's English was rife with malapropisms.

I remember one of my birthday parties as a boy. We had invited some of my friends, all boys. When my mom brought out the cake, she sang:

For he's a Hollywood fellow,
For he's a Hollywood fellow
For he's a Hollywood fellow...
Here her voice rose to the culminating verse:
Y eso digo yo (That's what I say).

My friends burst out laughing uncontrollably while I turned a hundred shades of pink. "Mom, it's 'He's a *jolly good* fellow.'" Mom just smiled and laughed along with the boys. She seemed to have no idea about "Happy birthday to you," or it just wasn't part of her ceremonial protocol. In fact, I have no recollection of my family singing the *Cumpleaños feliz* tune in the same melody as the English one until the 1970s. At other times my friends could barely understand her, like when, for example, she would say "Jeemereez creeckers" when I think she was trying to say, "Gee whiz," or "Jeesum Crow," or "Jiminy Cricket." Further on, I began to find her malapropisms, her Castilian pronunciation, and her Spanish-English wordplays not only interesting from a linguistic point of view, but charming. Such an odd-funny way of speaking; people would never say this openly, but no doubt that's what they thought.

No doubt the main language spoken on the ship they boarded—the USS *Galen L. Stone*, setting off from Palos de Moguer (Seville, Spain) to Philadelphia—was English. But Paco, Merche, and little Jorge spoke Spanish, pretending (I surmise) that language would not be a major problem for Mercedes. When they got to Philadelphia, off they went by train to Washington, DC. I wonder if my mom had begun to utter a few words in English on that trip; it took them three weeks from late April to mid-May in 1946. The *Galen L. Stone* was one of many "liberty ships" used for cargo and troop transportation during World War II. After the war, it was an ocean liner whose passengers consisted of thousands of European immigrants (the ones who managed to secure a ticket) eager to start a new life in America and just as impatient to leave behind so much destruction and suffering. I imagine—Imagination is as much a friend to me as Memory—a friend or higher-up in the U.S. diplomatic corps set up the trip for them. The official end of that second big war was September 1945, just a few months before they set sail. Expectations as well as uncertainties must have characterized their mood as they sallied westward across the Atlantic.

The circumstances of their arrival are something I can be sure of—I found out about it in an official State Department file on my father in the National Archives and Records housed in St. Louis, Missouri. According to correspondence between my father and the administrators of the U.S. Embassy in Madrid, as well as with the U.S. Department of State, my dad asked for an unpaid leave from his position at the Embassy. That's where I found his letter requesting a visa to the U.S. Yet while he was determined to leave Spain, he wasn't sure what exactly he would do when he got to his destination, thinking (naïvely) that due to his service to the government of his adopted country, surely someone would find something for him to do. How did he explain this to my mom? She just went along with him, psychologically and literally.

So, Paco set sail with his pretty wife Mercedes following closely behind, sometimes pushing him along. I can see them, all three, the Atlantic's wind in their faces, dreaming, each in their own way, of what was in store at the other end. She must have had faith in her Paco, as well as hope that they would be better off in the land of freedom and democracy. Learning the English language, along with all the other details of life—a place to live, a job, provisions, clothes—all those things would work themselves out, far better in the long run than living through Franco's reprisals and scarcity. In Spain people spoke the way she did, but now it was a language of oppression and dictatorship, which was not the idiom she was used to. Besides, she spoke French fluently after several years in France. No reason to be embarrassed about that.

There was a marked difference between the two of them in their aspirations. Clearly for Paco the land of liberty represented something of an Eden of the future, not only for the world, but for himself and his family. In that he was the typical European immigrant, espousing what he thought were "American values" in contrast to the turmoil and destruction of Europe in the wake of a near takeover by fascists elsewhere. In some ways, despite the defeat of Nazism, Europe had failed to see it coming. My mom sensed this as well, with all the travails of her father, and the fact that her beloved France had done virtually nothing to help him. There was no political disagreement on this. Yet for her there were other factors that defined her life, both before and after her arrival: the physical well-being of her family and her class pride. She had been reared in an atmosphere of social superiority, and she was going to do all she could to keep the appearance of her social privilege. Identity—it was this she both sought to preserve and to figure out. Mercedes thought of herself as a well-to-do woman who came from a fine family in Spain, married to a handsome man who would surely keep her in that superior position in the New World. She flaunted her husband's status, and her purpose in life was to be married to him—the faculty wife, the companion, the appendage. "Heee [with the guttural j sound in Spanish] ees so hansom, deesteengweesh professor." And that made her distinguished too. But it also made for tensions. My dad always made her feel uneducated, pointing out her errors in speaking and in writing: "*Escribes con letra de cocinera*" (You write like a cook), which referred to both her spelling and penmanship. Later in her life, well after his death, she tried her hand at writing, and it was not just because I encouraged her to do so—it was her idea, something of a creative urge she wanted to develop.

My father was the lucky one. While the U.S. diplomatic corps could not seem to find anything for him in Washington, he landed a job as an instructor of Spanish language at Dartmouth College, a perfect place perhaps

My mom, dad, and my brother George circa 1946

more for Mercedes than egalitarian Paco: an ivy-league institution attended by *la crème de la crème*. The location—Hanover, New Hampshire—must have seemed distant and strange to both of them, especially for my mom, the *manchega* (from La Mancha). She had been to France, but never to the New World. My dad's job was something temporary, indeed the employment letter made it clear that it would be for only fourteen months, at which point, he hoped, the diplomats would offer him something in foreign service in Washington. But no, that initial job of instructor of Spanish turned into a tenure track job, and later a position as distinguished professor at hifalutin Dartmouth. My mother was thrilled: it meant not only job security in an idyllic living place for her family, it also meant she might be able to look down on people like she did in La Mancha.

But as a famous Civil War–exile Spanish poet, Luis Cernuda, asks when he is offered a job teaching Spanish at Mt. Holyoke College in Massachusetts, "*¿Cómo serán los árboles aquellos?*" (I wonder what those trees are like). "*¡Dios mío!*" (My God!) she must have blurted out to Paco when she saw the first snow cover those trees. And later when she felt the subzero New Hampshire air make its way through her body and freeze her insides, the "Dios mío" must have turned into something like, "*¡Pero Paco ¿adónde me has llevado?!*" (Paco, where the devil have you taken me?) But with time, as Paco's job became more secure, not only did she get used to that bitter frigidity, she started to like it. In several of the photos of my mom recently arrived in the U.S., I see a happy and pretty woman eager to please and dying to show off. There she is on skis. Yes, that's Mercedes, a girl from the plains of La Mancha dressed in a heavy coat, earmuffs, a scarf, ski pants, ski boots, traversing a hill within walking distance from her home in Hanover, New Hampshire. And she's smiling from ear to ear. Indeed, my mother loved whiteness. And that's the dominant color of the several black-and-white photos of her in her ski outfit, surely taken by her proud husband.

My mom grew to love all that powdery, fluffy, cold purity. I think she truly enjoyed donning a fur (or fake fur) coat. She couldn't wait to tell her family in Hellín that she and Paco had made it to a paradisiacal winter wonderland. She enjoyed accompanying her two boys to the various winter events—ski meets, hockey games, ice skating trips.

The New England frigidity was all around, even in their social relations. Still, those were years of contentment at first, even knowing that their stay in these white and green surroundings might only be temporary. First, they lived in a college-owned apartment on South Park Street, and not much later they were able to buy a house on Dana Road off Wheelock Street, an easy walking distance from the college campus. By this time Mercedes had learned English, although her heavy Spanish accent was something of an impediment both to her and to the locals. As 1949 rolled around, her second son was born, and everything in her life should have been perfect.

But it wasn't. All those things of the past came back to scream otherwise, like her mental illness just after I was born. The experience of those "obuses" never left her memory. She was suspicious of strangers, particularly those whom we did not know who called us on the phone. Did she think our phone was tapped? Or that some evil person was listening to us with the intent of doing harm? When she answered a call from a poor soul who had dialed a wrong number, she would yell, "Thees eess a crock!" But all this was part of her charming quirkiness that turned into paranoia. My mom was enchantingly eccentric, and with her Spanish accent, she was also exotic. Few of us, not even my dad, pondered the possibility that the "crock" phone calls, later the objects of irrational obsessions, might come from her lived experiences. "*Paco, me llevas aquí a Siberia para luego abandonarme en un manicomio*" (Paco, you bring me here to Siberia just to dump me off in an insane asylum).

Siberia? A figure of speech. To those, like my mom, who have never been there, it conjures up a wasteland, the cold stillness of a place where political prisoners and crazy people are taken for their "crimes" or for non-conforming behavior.

Chapter 7

Mercedes' Mental Malady Revisited

Manicomio. In Spanish that means madhouse, a crude way of saying mental hospital or "retreat." I suspect that when she remembered her experience out loud, she was thinking of the first acceptation.

It was 1949, just three years after they set sail, the year of her institutionalization in Brattleboro. Much of the information in the mental hospital's anamnesis proved to be true from what I remember both of my parents saying about it. But like with most of these supposedly scientific hospital reports, there was much more to the story. Not that the report was inaccurate, it's that it didn't come from the knowledge, the context, or the psychological understanding of the events that led to Mercedes' mental illness.

There is no doubt that the Brattleboro Retreat was a nightmare for Mercedes, something out of a gothic novel. To the few times she spoke about it, that's what she said, *una pesadilla* (nightmare). A horrible dream is what I thought too. I didn't want to remember her incoherent descriptions of it until I was in my fifties. But her anamnesis case number 14619 changed my perception. A nightmare, yes, I'm certain it was, even though I was less than a year old when she was there. For my entire life I have been obsessed with the thought that the nightmare came as a consequence of my birth.

I think of my mom in those days as having been thrown into a snake pit. Growing up, I remember that no film terrified me more than *The Snake Pit*, starring Olivia de Havilland and adapted from a novel by Mary Jane Ward. It's about a woman diagnosed with schizophrenia who suffers a harrowing stay in a mental hospital in the 1950s. De Havilland's character personifies the ideal of female postwar beauty, grace, discretion, and submissiveness, but she hears voices in her head. She fails to recognize her recently wed husband, a kind man who commits her to the hospital when her behavior becomes uncontrollable. This attractive, pleasant woman acts strangely, and we don't know why—not unlike my mom after I was born. De Havilland didn't look like my mother, but she was what my mother aspired to be after she moved to the States.

As a product of the fifties, I wanted my mother to be like Olivia de Havilland—like the kind, well-mannered woman she played in many of her films and in this one too, except when she was crazy. Although Mary Jane Ward didn't want to admit it, her novel was autobiographical. Reading it well after I saw the movie for the first time, I was surprised by how different my reaction to the novel was in comparison to the film. Like the movie, the written version is an account of a woman's treatment for schizophrenia, along with that of her fellow incarcerated patients in the asylum. The layers of wards each serve a specific psychiatric function adequate to the needs of patients with various gradations of mental illness (schizophrenia, schizoid-paranoia, manic depression, neurosis A, neurosis B, psychosis Z). The author describes the relative ease and freedom enjoyed by the residents of some wards, as opposed to others where there is more constraint and where the nurses are chosen according to how much they can bench-press. In the end, the crazy lead lady gets cured—sort of.

All this was in the film too, but for some reason (probably my age and circumstances), it terrified me when I saw it in my early teens. It was all I could do not to think of my mother living with all those diabolical witchlike figures, the residents of the nuthouse. It was a horrific fairy tale, a nightmare. The novel shows how poorly the mentally ill are treated: unsympathetic nurses, doctors more interested in their own reputations than the well-being of their patients, a therapeutic system that treats people with disorders as if they were prisoners. However, as a youngster, I thought the film was something out of the Brothers Grimm. My sympathy was with Virginia, the character played by de Havilland. Everyone else was an obstacle to her cure, which is what I was hoping for. The ordinal numbers for the wards were magical categories of levels of achievement. In the lower numbers, the characters were almost normal. But those in the higher numbered wards were like monsters, some in straitjackets or shackles, angry, screaming and struggling to be free.

I will never forget a sequence that made me think of my mother Mercedes as I imagined her in the Brattleboro Retreat, that black and white image of a "snake pit" that gave both the novel and the movie its title. It's one of film history's most vividly creepy images: in one of the highest-numbered wards, the one where the patients, including Virginia, barely know where they are, some are weeping, some smile or laugh as if they had seen something only they were able to see. The floor of this ward turns into a hole in the ground that widens into a cavern as the camera rises to give us a picture of the entire panorama. What we're looking at turns into an entire society of strange beings, something out of Hieronymus Bosch's hell, an enormous underground dwelling; from out of the bowels of an underground cave of insanity we can see it all and be relieved we're not there, terrified that we or someone we know—like my mother—might end up there. I didn't want my mom to be in that pit. More precisely, I didn't want my mom to have been there.

But let me look at this with the eyes of someone no longer in his teens, no longer terrified that his mom was confined in a house with crazy monsters. For the record, my mother received the best possible care available at that time, the medical attention provided to a New England elite. While by today's standards the hospital staff was unsophisticated about the life circumstances of people from other cultures, at least their intentions were humane, with the exception of the ice packs, and it's hard to refute that she left the place in better shape than when she arrived. Many years later as I read the assessments of her problems offered by all the different actors in the story, including my father's, I marvel at how real-seeming they are, I recognize my mom: that's her as she talks about her communist brother, as she complains about the gas they gave her during delivery, as she physically resists a couple of the nurses, and pulls one of them down before they "place her in pack." Yes, she is recognizable to me; Memory (or memory of my mom's memory) has not let me down, even though there are some events and circumstances in the medical record that are new to me. But all in all, there is nothing in the pages of the dossier that surprises me.

So, here is my section-by-section, blow-by-blow commentary, correction, and clarification of the official record of my mom's first bout with psychosis.

Even that word is problematic. My mother's psychiatrists' confusion as to what term best describes her illness says much about the strangeness not only of this case in particular, but about mental illness in general, as much then as today. However, I have no question that there was something wrong with Mercedes. And the anamnesis testifies to that.

Considering her background before 1949, the sections titled "Family Background," "Personal History," "Education," and "Marital History" spark a fundamental question about where all this information is coming from. Yes, as I often tell my students: consider the source. And the answer here is not difficult. The anamnesis tells us plainly: it's the "informant." That means my father, or as they call him on numerous occasions, "the husband." What I read in this medical record is my dad's assessment of his wife's history. But naturally, as with any history (including the one, reader, you have in your hands), the assessment is shaped by the one who tells it. As I read the travails of my mom's distress about the betrayal of my father by his colleagues at Dartmouth, it's clear to me that my dad was talking as much about himself as about his wife.

When I was clearing out my mom's possessions when she moved from New Hampshire to Missouri in her later years, I found a letter by Professor Alvin Pianca to my dad dated 1946. The tone was friendly, helpful, and collegial. He said he looked forward to meeting my father and the family in person, and, as a suggestion, he advised that my dad bring along some of the bare necessities that were hard to come by in certain parts of the United States after the war, things like bedsheets, toiletries, and warm clothing to keep them comfortable in the New England winters. It's surprising that here too in the land of plenty where there had been no war, here in what was rapidly becoming the consumer capital of the world, there was postwar scarcity. Despite Pianca's initial helpfulness, this was the man who would, for God knows what reason, urge the Department to dismiss my father. As a professor in a languages department myself, I know all too well how things work in academia. There is an official reason the department changed its mind about Francisco Ugarte. But the most compelling explanation of the rejection of my father is the machinations of pride and hierarchies that persist in the deceptively genteel circles of life among the faculty, well portrayed in *Who's Afraid of Virginia Woolf?*

The official explanation might be, probably was, that he was not sufficiently qualified to be a professor at Dartmouth. His degree at the Universidad Complutense of Madrid in 1935 was in *Derecho* (Jurisprudence). It was not seen, as "the informant" claims, as equivalent to a PhD. The Ivy League culture of Dartmouth necessitated a first-rate faculty with the most prestigious degrees. How can a man with a foreign law degree teach Spanish language and literature along with courses on the "Great Works of the Humanities"? He was not Dartmouth material, as was Alvin Pianca, who was a Dartmouth grad, class of 1922 (regardless of his southern Italian background). Lots of inbreeding at Dartmouth, and my dad was an outsider; no one in the Ugarte-Precioso clan had been to Dartmouth, or any suchlike institution. Paco's a good man, says Professor Pianca, but he is not qualified, and he got a certain Professor Arce to go along with his move to run my father into the ground.

Here is the murkier situation: Pianca told him to situate himself behind someone who would protect him. This was how it worked. Of course my father reacted to this negatively. I can attest to it because it was in his character: He was Basque. He would be no one's lackey. "Why is it always best to be financially independent, Miguel?" he would ask me, as if it were a question on a test. The punch line was *Para no depender de ningún cabrón* (So you don't have to depend on the whims of a son-of-a-bitch). It seems obvious the *cabrón* was Pianca. If my father was going to be promoted, it would be on his own merit. A society of patronage was the one he left behind, a world in which the strong-man protector rules, with a *caudillo* (chief) like Franco (or Mussolini, Hitler, or Salazar) deciding who would advance and who would not. And this experience, here in the land of freedom and meritocracy, had put a huge dent in his high estimation of the inherent American sense of fairness.

But the mistake—as my father himself admits, echoing the opinion of one of the psychiatrists—was to carry the woes of his precarious work situation into the safety, tranquility, and familial happiness of his new home. I imagine dinner conversations in those days just before I was born as Mercedes put Jorgito to bed: "Paco, I told you. You believe everything they tell you. *Cándido* (innocent, naïve). They are listening to us. They know about Artemio in Russia; they think we're communists. They know my father was sentenced to death. If you don't watch out, they'll expel us or put us in jail." In the long run, several decades later, after I too had become involved in complex dramas of tenure and promotion within academia, I think my mother was right, while not exactly in the specific sense, certainly in the overall sense of *Así es, Paco* (That's just the way it is, Paco).

And my father would reply by going on about what his colleagues were saying without reacting directly to my mother's politicization of the family dilemma. What then of my mother's reactions to all this faculty intrigue? I can only speculate. I'm sure that her devotion to her husband put her on his side, that his professional travails made her sad and defensive. This eternally admiring faculty wife was charming to my father's colleagues, friendly and accommodating to their spouses. But like *Virginia Woolf*'s Martha, there was much more to my mother than the stand-by-your-man wife. She had travails of her own, axes to grind, suspicions, rancor, and bad faith. Who were these people who were trying to denigrate her husband? And why? Leaving those questions to the arbitrariness of life and the strangeness of the new land was not in her character. To her, there was no such thing as arbitrariness; there were always forces at work, forces against which it was supremely difficult to mount a defense. These people were out to get her husband, just as the Franquistas and the ones before them had been out to get her father and his freethinking associates. Their ideological war of words had led to law suits against Artemio Sr. that ruined his social and financial security, so why couldn't this happen in the so-called land of freedom?

When my mom was a prepubescent girl who no doubt had heard vague talk in her household about the calumnies against her father, much of it was incomprehensible to her. *Why were they against him?* her inner voice asked. Probably because they had antidemocratic, perhaps fascistic, tendencies. They were terrified of the kind of progressive changes her father and those of his ilk were calling for, such as less Church influence in government and society, public rather than exclusively parochial education, land reform, and free elections. But I do not remember my mother as a woman actively pushing for these kinds of changes in her life. Yes, she was conflicted by them, as well she should have been. But it was also true that she and her family had profited precisely from the closed society that her father had decried, a landowning structure comprised of large estates in the hands of the few. My great-grandfather, Artemio Sr.'s dad, had deforested the lands of La Mancha and had made a fortune from it.

There are discrepancies among my mother's siblings on how they perceive the family wealth: most say that Artemio Sr. had simply taken another path; he wanted to remain among the wealthy, but he would do it his own way. His daughters saw that as admirable, but what they were not willing to concede was their status, an aristocratic *savoir faire*, an assumed superiority in comparison to *las muchedumbres* (the masses, the riffraff). Artemio's son, the *benjamín* (youngest) of the family, sided with that riffraff and became a communist at age eighteen. But even between my mother and her sister Marina I detected disagreement on how to treat those unable to enjoy the benefits of their class. My aunt was empathetic, generous, and (at least on the surface) kind to the less fortunate. But my mother was suspicious of them. They wanted what the family had; you could never trust them; they're uncouth, slippery. "Watch out for the bad ones, Paco," she would say.

Here is what anamnesis 14619 does not say: in my mother's eyes, Pianca's Puerto Rican wife, Linda, was less *linda* (pretty) than Puerto Rican, which for my mom meant she was a native of a former Spanish colony, subaltern. One might wonder how a woman with such an egalitarian father and a communist brother could have these retrograde attitudes. But given Spanish sensibilities—a certain national arrogance and disregard for people of the colonies, even more pronounced among my mom and dad's generation—this is not hard to fathom. No wonder Linda's Italian husband (probably Sicilian) was seeking to do my father in: he was envious. In New England at that time, Italians were the Latinos of today. Paco was tall, light-skinned, and Basque. Pianca was envious of his looks, according to Mercedes. More importantly, as the psychiatrists suggested, my mom was associating the ill treatment of her husband by the Department with her father's hardships at the hands of jealous and fearful people.

Or it's also possible this was my father's projection. Not the part having to do with social class—my father was proud of his Basque heritage, which means he believed democracy and equality were second nature. Social equality is part of the Basque way of being; that's just the way things are organized in *Euskadi* (the Basque Country). But the part having to do with politics is another matter. They did not have a television at that time, although they listened to the radio. By 1949, the House Un-American Activities Committee was in full swing, and Joe McCarthy was just getting started. Was my dad afraid? My sense is that he was not as concerned about the political connections of his wife's family as he was about his professional reputation at the college. For it was Mercedes' father and brother who had suffered the abuses and arbitrariness of political-social circumstance. Not my father. The Ugarte patriarch, my grandfather Javier, might have been crazy as a loon, but much too interested in his own well-being to enter into ideological battles. Indeed, my father was the protected one. The U.S. political establishment of the 1930s loved Francisco, a man in his twenties who spoke English fluently. Due to his perspicacity, hard work, and self-reliance—a more true-blooded American immigrant I can't think of—he managed to land a job at the U.S. Embassy in Madrid while working on his law degree. To this day, my assessment of his intellect and mental acumen emerges from his keen ability to learn languages. For a Spaniard of that time, to speak and write in elegant turns of phrase is not only an accomplishment, it is an indication my dad was intellectually worthy, even though his credentials did not provide hard evidence of that worthiness.

I surmise that the political references to persecution in the anamnesis are my mom's. And significantly, it is those political aspects of her "complaint," as the doctors called it, that got her into trouble. It was her persecution complex; she was hearing voices. Not only did the bad guys want to go after her and her family for their communist tendencies, they thought she had anarchist and fascist connections as well. But again, as she says—and I smiled knowingly when I read it—"fascists we very sure weren't."

I imagine that my father or the transcriber of the narrative of my mother's life got a few things wrong; probably the transcriber, because I don't think, for example, that my father would have told his interviewer that Mercedes' father was condemned to death in 1936. Yes, as we in the family knew all along, his accusers sought the death penalty, but not at the beginning of Franco's insurrection (1936), as the anamnesis says, but at the end of it, with the Victory of the Forces of Spanish Order, as they named it, and a return to its Catholic identity (1939). There is also a mention that he was forced out of Spain with "the turn of events" in that country, implying it happened with the war, but the reality is that it happened before that. I imagine my father provided details about a pre-Franco dictatorship that the compilers may have seen as superfluous. There are other inconsistencies, inaccuracies, and proverbial wait-a-minutes in the record, but as I attempt to reconstruct the life of my mother Mercedes, my intention is not just to set the record straight. With the help of my travel companion, Memory, I want to try to reimagine her life and her circumstances, and this attempt will probably fall short of accuracy. But accuracy often lies too. Again, I remain loyal to my mother in her wonderful aphorism: "Could be true and not have happened."

Still, there are occurrences and observations that the compilers of my mother's life (my father, the psychiatrists, the nurses, and now myself) can agree on. It's a question of priorities: which occurrences and observations are most crucial to enter into the unsettled mind of Mercedes? For me, the fact she married her uncle is always looming over all the other events of her life. But then again, maybe that's just one factor among a slew of others.

Memory cannot tell me the time I learned about the blood relationship, so I'll speculate it was my father who told me at around age twelve, probably so that when or if my Spanish family members made a fuss about it, I would be prepared. By that time, I had already been (back) to Spain twice, but I was so young that such things would have passed through me without notice. In any case, since then I have thought a great deal about the consequences and permutations: my grandfather was also my mom's grandfather, my dad's brothers were my mom's uncles, my beloved Auntie Marina, whom I remember at times as the mother I wish I'd had, was my cousin, and the "real" (for lack of a better word) cousins were also my nephews and nieces, my grandmother was also my aunt, and my father was also my great uncle. Many years later I read Jeffrey Eugenides's *Middlesex*, the epic tale of a couple joined not only by marriage but also by the fact that they were born of the same mother and father. Remarkable in the novel how that taboo became a relatively insignificant detail of the marriage as their lives together developed once they had moved from Greece to the U.S. That's what happened to Paco and Mercedes. Their blood relationship became something of an untoward detail of their lives. Yes, America is the land of opportunity, a place you can reinvent yourself, get rid of excess baggage, pretend certain unpleasantries either don't exist or they're just not worth introspection. In America you begin with a blank slate, sometimes a new name, a new identity. And since the majority of the Americans you will deal with have no idea where you come from, full speed ahead. My dad was about to construct a new persona and a new career as he crossed the Atlantic. His silence on the issue of his blood relationship with his wife reveals as much about him as about Mercedes' mental illness at Brattleboro. True, Mercedes suffered from hypersensitivity, excitability, paranoia, and occasional melancholy before she was married (although that part of her life is the most unfamiliar to me), but we can be certain that the marriage to her uncle exacerbated all of this. Reader, look over the few mentions of this fact in the anamnesis. How could the experts dismiss it, or not give it more attention? That is, not until we get to Mr. Czatt's assessment: "[There is] the fact also that she was afraid her child was going to be some sort of monster because of the congenital heredity." Interesting that Mr. Czatt is the only "Mr." among a slew of "Dr."s.

Memory, here you are again, edging me in the direction of Mercedes' history and being. This I remember. My mom used the word monster on more than one occasion in reference to what I might have been: Frankenstein? Godzilla? A giant Iguana? Subnormal (the politically incorrect term in Spain for someone with a disability)? A zombie creeping out of the screen of *The Snake Pit*? The image my mother painted of me that I recall most vividly is when she told me about the nightmarish days immediately after my birth. She worked herself into a frenzy relating how she imagined my grotesque face, one eye much larger than the other and teeth growing out of my nose. Memory and I are having a good laugh now; we both agree I wasn't that ugly. Look at the photographs, Miguel is not so grotesque. But Memory also knows what a lasting impression that monster image made on me in my childhood through adolescence and even after.

How could my mother consider her Miguelito a monster? We'll see.

Chapter Eight

Faculty Wife

A monster I was not, although at times, I remember as a child and as an adolescent, my mother would act out her dark moods, surreal and terrifying memories of her stay in the Brattleboro snake pit. Her eyes would grow large, her mouth contorted, and she would say something like, "They say you had teeth growing out of your nose" or *"Monstruo, Miguel, eso me dijeron"* (A Monster, Miguel, that's what they told me). Pure Mercedes drama, which was something between grotesque and hilarious because I was living proof that whoever told her I would be a monster needed only to take a look at Miguelito when he was a week old. Still, it was not something to address to your child later on when he was nine or ten, not as a vulnerable adolescent either. She should have said, after the bit about her monster child, that in reality I turned out *beaux* and *grand*, as in that African melody from Côte d'Ivoire. *"Mama disait que j'étais beaux. Mama disait que j'étais grand."* As I listen at age sixty-something to this beautiful song by Kouame Sereba, I think of my mom—fondly, tenderly, lovingly. The song says, "Mama used to say I was pretty and great" or beautiful and big, depending on how one wants to translate those key words. Yes, to leave my mom's assessment of her second-born son, Miguel—baptized Michael Frank—as a Halloween caricature is not accurate. There's always another story.

There is a family photo of Mercedes and little Miguelito taken about a year after my birth, just two or so years after she had begun her new "career" as a faculty wife at Dartmouth, and several months after her stay at the "Retreat." My father is in the background. It is not a portrait in the classical sense of a family on display for the sake of posterity or self-importance. There are plenty of those in my family, but they are not nearly as interesting as this partial candid. I say partial because, while my mom was posing for the camera, as she often did, my dad in the background seemed utterly indifferent. For me, at age one, surely the whole event was a big question mark.

Mercedes, Michael, *"Heess hair was so whooayeet."* Paco in background. Hanover, New Hampshire; circa 1950

We are outside. The picture must have been taken in the spacious yard encircling the apartment building in Hanover where we lived in the early fifties. In the foreground my mom is kneeling on the grass and holding me by her side up to the camera as if I were her trophy. I'm squinting because she had planted us under the sun in compliance, no doubt, with the photographer's directions. I am the center of the photo. My face and hair blend naturally with an invisible sun lording over the scene and making its presence felt with my half-shut eyes, the light-green grass in need of water, and my shirtless dad in the background sitting in a lawn chair.

My mom is the radiant one. Her smile is contagious: it's genuine, it's happy. She was always photogenic, but here she emanates authenticity and wholesomeness. The smile exposes her teeth, beautifully surrounded by a near-perfect mouth and the signature Ugarte larger-than-normal nose (she would have said aristocratic; I prefer Basque); her dark eyes and coiffed black hair are in smart contrast with the brightness of the smile. Her upper body is partly visible as she props me up. Everything in the photo is light—all, that is, except my mom, although the shades of her skin, her expressive brown eyes and pretty black hair make the lightness even more vibrant in comparison. My left hand is clasped shut. In my vague memory (or a dream?) I recall that I was eating a cookie. Could it be true? I'm not sure anyone can remember something that happened at age one. She is wrapping her left arm around me, not as much in an embrace as in firm support of something she wants to show off. She is wearing a blouse over a yellow tee shirt. I am dressed in a blue tee shirt and red striped jumper with an apple in the middle of my chest just about where the heart is.

My father is sitting behind us to the left in a green lawn chair that blends with the grass; he draws his left hand up toward his face as if to wipe his brow. Although you can't quite see it, his right hand is holding what must be a book. His posture is somewhat slouched, a typical pose when he was tired. There is no way of knowing, but circumstantial evidence suggests he has something on his mind. His manic-depressive psychosis does not show in the photo, but it later became clear. Although at the time this was taken, he had won his battle to stay on the faculty at Dartmouth, still he had to continue to prove himself to the community of scholars. At this particular moment he seems uninspired by his wife's pride in their creation, her relief, her happiness in the wake of those dark weeks immediately after my birth. For Mercedes, her little Miguelito was not only normal, he was light-skinned. Fancy that.

Years later, after I had become an activist against racial discrimination and injustice and against the Vietnam War, I was mortified when my mother addressed herself to whomever would lend an ear, announcing that her second child's hair was not only blond, it was white. What I heard was that she thought I looked regal, pure, icy, waspy, colorless, and for those reasons, a cut above the rest. All this embarrassed me to no end. I confess it made me feel ashamed. Perhaps it shouldn't have; she was just a mother proud of her son's looks. *"Mama disait que j'étais blanc."* No, not exactly. But she did say,

"Heess hair was so whooayeet. Pure whooayeet. My leetel Maicol." When she spoke about me, she called me "Maicol." When she spoke to me, she called me Miguel.

She would talk about my blond-white hair often, whenever she reminisced about my childhood. As I ponder her delight in her second son's whiteness, I suspect her object of pride was all about her, her sense of self or lack thereof. Despite my father's unbridled enthusiasm about coming to the United States, for her, in her mid-thirties, in all her Spanish class privilege, coming to the land that welcomed immigrants was a step down. I suspect the only times my mom had seen or dealt with black people were during a few months in Washington, DC—when she had just arrived in the U.S. with her husband—and during a short stint in Chicago where my dad went to the university to take courses to fulfill the expectations of the people at Dartmouth who were judging his lack of academic preparation. As I was growing up, there was only one black family in Hanover. In my mother's mind, blacks were like gypsies—marginal, unsightly, untrustworthy, and dangerous. And she was not the only Spaniard to make that association—García Lorca did as well in his famous New York poem, "The King of Harlem." But for my mom, unlike Lorca, any kind of association with marginal beings was not a good idea. And what made her prejudices more palpable and fraught was that there was always a lurking possibility that she herself might be perceived as someone akin to the racial other. Her own coloring, while obviously Caucasian, was dark, a little on the olive side. In certain circles of New England, they called it "swarthy," and it wasn't good. That's why she fell for Paco Ugarte, the Basque, the northerner, whose skin color, blue-green eyes, tall stature, education, and worldliness set him apart at once from her as well as from ordinary Spaniards. He was unlike ordinary Americans too, and quite unlike blacks. Yes, for Mercedes, skin color, appearance, stature, image, were all of utmost importance.

But the color of my hair changed; starting who knows when—around age five it got darker. By second grade it was brown. I remember a scary incident in second grade that makes me think today that the residual effects of my birth and Mercedes' ideation that I would be born a monster still lingered. For a reason unclear to me, I had something against my second-grade teacher; she was old, stern, and critical. Something I can't put my finger on happened in the classroom closet where the children put their coats: the teacher's rebuke, a grimace, a shrill voice scared and saddened me. I decided the next day I would not go back to school. This was during those enviable small-town days when, even at age six or seven, kids could walk to school if it wasn't too far. So instead of going to my second-grade classroom, I went to Stoney's, an all-purpose store that sold hot tamales, peanut butter cups, Cokes, and other unhealthy treats for pennies. I spent my milk money on these delights, and lucky for me, every Monday the Dartmouth ROTC students marched "as to war" in the Dartmouth soccer practice fields, which were directly behind Stoney's. Playing hooky could not have been better: after my fill of those sugary delicacies, I would march along with the soldier-students until it was time to go home.

It did not take long for Paco and Mercedes to get wind of this. Who did I think I was fooling? They were not happy, but especially unhappy was my mom—more like hysterical. I can see her expressions today: the typical pained face, eyes wide open conveying urgency and impending danger, disbelief. How could her son, at one time so "whooayeet," do such a dark thing? Her overreaction was due, I conjecture, to her embarrassment at having to talk to the school principal, but just as much to her lingering suspicion that Miguelito was not as angelic as she thought, that the *relación sanguínea* was coming back to haunt.

"Reeform school. *Allí acabarás*" (That's where you'll end up). Maybe Memory is deceiving me, but I recall that she told me she was about to call a school for juvenile delinquents to make arrangements for sending me there. Surely, she must have added the big "if": *if* I pulled something like that again—but I don't remember it. All I remember is my horror that I would be off to reform school within a couple of days.

Decades later: I asked my mom in Spanish, "Mom, remember when you and Dad wanted to send me to reform school?" And her response was laughter. *Ay sí. ¡Qué miedo tenías! Eras tan inocente* (Oh yes. You were so afraid. You were so innocent). Innocent until proven guilty, and clearly, I was proven guilty. But, as I told her, it was she who was not innocent; she put a wedge in my self-confidence and sense of security. Returning the laughter, I

Mercedes: Light and Dark   103

told her I was going to send her the bill for all my counseling sessions. So I guess I wasn't so "whooayeet," Mom. Again she laughed.

I'm portraying Mercedes as something of a racist. She was, but we have to put that in context. She was a product of her times with lots of hierarchies and prejudices added in. Those who boast of being unscathed by the prejudices of their time might want to take another look at themselves. I don't exclude myself. Another case in point is that of Mom's relation with Teresa Marín-Padilla and her husband Miguel, a promising young doctor and researcher at Dartmouth Medical School. The Marín-Padilla family was one of maybe two families who spoke Spanish at home, like us. The head of the other family was from Córdoba—in the south of Spain—and had family acquaintances in Hellín. Just what my mom and dad wanted—someone they could talk to. Teresa, or Tere, as her family called her, was everything Linda Pianca of earlier years was not, with the exception that she was Puerto Rican. But Tere was of a new generation; a scientist in her own right, she was not one to follow along dutifully in the line of all the faculty wives at Dartmouth. She had a career, and she was good at what she did, this in an all-male college atmosphere. And my mom found her fascinating. They came for visits utterly unannounced, usually on Sundays, such a Spanish thing to do. Announcements are for people who do not enjoy intimacy, laughter, casual everyday behavior, and most of all loud—very loud—voices. My mom would often tell Paco that she needed to go to the store because at any moment the Marín-Padillas would come by. *Allí están* (There they are), she declared as my brother and I were watching an NFL game. And my dad would stop everything he was doing to receive them with open arms, embraces, the warmth they missed from home. And of course, it was about a shared language and a shared culture. Miguel was familiar with the artist who had painted a portrait of Mercedes' father, Romero de Torres, because Torres was also from Córdoba. What a mix of accents—my dad's professorial, albeit loud and animated, Castilian Spanish, Tere with cadences straight out of the Caribbean, and my mom's Manchegan style, lots of diminutives, and even more drama. *Ay Tere, pero qué guapa* (Oh Tere, how pretty you are) as she ran into the kitchen in search of whatever was ready to serve.

Yet it's also true that my mom viewed Tere with a lingering suspicion. She was Puerto Rican: How could she be a doctor? And even more insidious in her warped classist and racist mind, her suspicion had to do with Tere's complexion, dark like her own. Miguel's wife emanated an African descent that made my mother harken to the days in Madrid when the only African women she had seen were in the theater. Indeed, she loved Josephine Baker, who performed several times in Madrid for adoring Madrileños like my mom, probably my dad too, who no doubt thought that Baker was something like the Second Coming (with bananas). Exotic and sexy as sin. So how could someone of the same extraction as Josephine Baker be a doctor?

I was embarrassed by my mom's attitudes about whiteness, but at the same time, I wanted her to be white too, in the sense of being normal, like my friends' moms, the ones whose dads were professors, doctors, or administrators at Dartmouth: elegant, poised, a little superior. Dare I admit that I wanted her to be blond? God forbid. A heavy Spanish accent did not lend itself to that. I did not want to feel out of place, much less ashamed of my own mother, a woman I saw every day. I saw her more than I saw my dad, who was always off at the office doing and teaching important things. I respected him more than I respected my mom.

Flash forward to many years later, well after I had stopped feeling ashamed. In fact, I came to embrace my mother's "otherness" in a way that made me, her son, also seem exotic, a bit more interesting than normal. I was happy to introduce my mother to the people around me. She had moved to Missouri—or more accurately, I had moved her kicking and screaming—and I decided to throw a birthday party for her when she turned ninety. In my department, there was no scarcity of non-native English speakers, particularly Latin Americans, and my mom was a big hit with them. The party I hosted for her was a huge success—lots of wine and champagne, food from the Spanish and Portuguese-speaking world (*tapas* galore), and lots of naughty funny talk. My mother kept smiling. If there's one thing she loved, it was being the center of attention. And she kept making references to me as if I were "available" (which I was not), as she called me "Miguel, el Superior." Ay Ay Ay. That time she did embarrass me, but not the way she did when I was a boy. From that moment on, my department chair, the late Flore Zephir, called me (with a big smile on her face) "Miguel, el Superior."

When I was a boy, my mother and father dragged me along to some of their college gatherings—lectures, receptions, discussions with students. I hated them: utterly boring, my father ranting on about God knows what and my mom speaking a mixture of Spanish and bad English with her characteristic drama and hyperbolic gestures. I remember one occasion in particular. It was an event that embarrassed me perhaps more than any other: an enactment of a scene from *Romeo and Juliet* in which—I have no idea why—my mom played Juliet and my dad Romeo, both decked out in Elizabethan costume. I was absolutely mortified that my dad's bulging private parts were showcased by the tight Shakespearean outfit he was wearing. Or was it Italian? After all, the play is set in Verona. All I wanted to do was run away. But now, about fifty-plus years later, I have reconsidered that memory. What was at that time humiliating, today seems wonderfully endearing. Remarkable how your ideas about your parents can change as you get older. The enactment was of the famous masked ball scene when Romeo and Juliet first meet and kiss in an ever so chaste way:

Romeo: If I profane with my unworthiest hand
This holy shrine, the gentle sin is this:
My lips, two blushing pilgrims, ready stand
To smooth that rough touch with a tender kiss.

To which Juliet replies:

Good pilgrim, you do wrong your hand too much,
Which mannerly devotion shows in this:
For saints have hands that pilgrims' hands do touch
And palm to palm is holy palmers' kiss.

I was around ten, and I remember having to witness them rehearsing this scene at home before, during, and after dinner. I hated it. They dragged me to the performance. I begged them not to force me to go, but I'm pretty sure it was my mother who insisted. She would be in her element, showing off her dramatic skills in a language not her own. I was embarrassed by it at home, but more so in public. I recall covering my eyes. And she butchered the language of Shakespeare in a way that made it—already unfamiliar to the ears of any American in the mid-twentieth century—sound utterly incomprehensible. To me, and I imagined to virtually all the people listening to her, some forty of them, she was speaking the language of an extraterrestrial. She got the inflections wrong, all her vowels were Spanish, not English, and every time she said "hand," she sounded like she was about to spit. And her eyes were open wide, way too wide (did they forget the masks?). Her gestures were exaggerated as she raised her arm and hand, waiting for the "palmers' kiss," which was actually a touch. The ups and downs of her tone, to me, a boy of ten, all seemed grotesque, as in "Oh . . . gross!" And there was my father, dignified by comparison, or trying to look that way. Although he had mastered the "King's English," he still had an accent that made his speech sound, as linguists might call it, "hypercorrect." That is, proper but slightly unnatural.

My dad had tried to coach her; in fact, I remember him correcting her often, not just for this Shakespearean scene but in virtually all occasions that required clear communication with non-Spanish speakers, and in small-town New England of the late forties and fifties, that meant just about everybody. But the Romeo and Juliet bit was a big success, or so they let on. Everyone applauded, and Paco and Mercedes loved the accolades—my dad showing off his Shakespearean English skills and my mom her passionate romance with the Romeo she had fallen for. A few college students came over to me to tell me it must be fantastic to have a mom and dad like that. My mother lived for those kinds of experiences. Today that performance makes me think of that memorable film of Florence Foster Jenkins, the would-be opera singer whom no one dared tell she sounded horrible. But then again, my mom was different from Florence Foster Jenkins, who sounded like a cat in heat. I sense Mercedes knew deep down that she was pronouncing the words wrong. The Shakespearean show wasn't nearly as embarrassing as I thought. I was the mortified one; no one but me. She performed as Juliet beautifully. She was pretty, indeed desirable. I'm sure the students were attracted to her in all their longing for anything female. This took place well before Dartmouth became coeducational (my dad died before this monumental change).

More than anything, as I grow older, that performance conveys that my mom was deeply in love with my dad. And for Mercedes, the thought of representing that love by acting like a young girl, a teenager who had just met the love of her life in a masked ball, could not have been more fulfilling. In this she went far beyond her role as faculty wife. Today I'm convinced that her love for my father throughout her life, from the time in Hellín when she first laid eyes on him, was absolutely genuine.

Another jump to the future, a few years after she had moved to Missouri—I bought her a copy of *Romeo and Juliet* in a used book store. When I gave it to her at age eighty-nine, I asked if she remembered acting in that scene for a group of Dartmouth students and professors, and she said she did, but not well. As I write I'm holding that very copy; in between page thirty and thirty-one I find a postcard, an insert requesting a subscription to *TV Guide*. And surrounding the printed lettering is her handwriting saying in Spanish, "Miguel says I should write. It's hard to explain sensations—why do that? I can only say that we all know we're going to die, and to arrive at eighty-six [here she crosses out eighty-six and replaces it with eighty-nine] and to write, isn't that sublime [the same word in Spanish]?" God knows what she meant by that—maybe not even God knows. All I can do is conjecture. Of course, at age eighty-nine she was thinking of death, but I find what she says about the sublime not only curious, it's characteristic of her because she always loved hyperbole. It also indicates to me that perhaps she was still feeling a love for her husband that, even well after his death, she remembered as "sublime." But surely that must be my projection. I have no idea what she meant by "sublime," although I do know she loved her Paco.

So much so, that in the light and darkness of all she had been through in Spain, she allowed that love to get the better of her. My mother was deeply jealous of many of the women who entered into my father's life. There was an ongoing argument between them, suspicious as she was that he was two-timing. The first suspect was my aunt Maruja, her sister by a second marriage. I know she worked at the Embassy with my dad, but I have no idea in what circumstances. I imagine it must have been as a secretary or stenographer. The topic of Maruja came up often. I must have been about seven, I think, when we got a recording in the mail from Madrid, one of those recorded telegrams. It was the voices of Maruja and her husband Victor telling my mom and dad how much they missed them, that things were great in Spain, much better than a few years ago, and that they had very fond memories of those years when Paco was at the Embassy. My mom did not react well. The recording upset her, and my father's reaction was something like, "*Eso ya pasó*" (That happened a while ago). At times Memory lets me down, because I was way too young to remember this accurately, let alone understand it. But what I was led to believe later on was that indeed my father had been attracted to Maruja, and he apologized for it. Later, the more I thought about it and the more closely I looked into my father's diaries, the more convinced I am that both Maruja and he acted on those desires. The issue did not go away for my mom. Maybe that was the origin of her jealousy, but today I don't think so. If it weren't Maruja, it would have been someone else. Subsequent arguments, really dramatic and loud ones, were about my mother's accusations of my father for his "interest" in someone pretty.

Maybe I'm naïve, but I can't imagine my dad sneaking into the guest room of a young Spanish student (a woman in her twenties) who was staying at our house. But Mercedes did accuse him of just that; it got so bad that she called her a *furcia* (whore). I do remember that scene; I was there listening, the three of them, my mom and dad with the young lady—her name was Inés—in the middle mingling close to a staircase that led to the bedrooms of our house on Dana Road. I think I had just come in from the yard. My mom was yelling in Spanish and the word she used, *furcia*, was something I had never heard, but I figured it out from the context and from the poor student's reaction: utter humiliation and indignation, as the tears streamed from her eyes. My dad tried unsuccessfully to remedy it all by forcefully telling my mom that she was inventing this. He was as humiliated as the young coed. My mom had a knack for making everyone feel embarrassed. That's how I felt then and at many other moments in my life. Today I'm not sure if all this has to do with my own curiosity or a necessity for her to let people know that she too was alive, that she too had resentments, anxieties, feelings that were unacknowledged.

Today in the twenty-first century, with all the talk of "me too" and the ongoing reality of all those lecherous professors lusting after students, giving promises of good grades or something else, I question my own attitude of doubt regarding my father's possible infidelity. Not with female students, because Dartmouth was all male, but maybe with someone else. After all, he killed himself. Was it for guilt? But with wrenching introspection and all my attempts to set the workings of Memory into motion, my conclusion is that if my father was tempted by the allures of other women, and I'm sure he was, I don't think he acted on those enticements—my dad was simply not that kind of guy. Am I naïve? As many Spaniards say, women too, when asked if they are married or attached, "*Casado/a pero no muerto/a*" ([I'm] married but not dead). My mom never said anything like that, but I know her fear that Paco would act on his attraction to other women made her anxious: "Paco, why you talk to that woman so much?"

Yes, my mom's jealousies persisted even after my dad died. My mom and I were in Campello in the mid-1990s, close to Alicante where my dad had bought a condominium facing the Mediterranean on the Muchavista Beach. My mother was in her early eighties. Campello was and remains a highly frequented area in the summer, so that cafés and restaurants were filled. We were enjoying ourselves with family and friends: my aunt Marina and her daughter (named Mercedes of course) with her husband Juanjo, as well as a young couple from Madrid (Armando and Mavi) whom I had known for a while. We were in a beachside café, a lovely evening, enjoying conversation and refreshment of various kinds. As usual, my mom had to be the center of attention, and her younger sister was all too happy to appear a bit more dignified by comparison, since by then my mom was showing early signs of dementia, a dementia not the least bit annoying at that time, because it gave her license to say outrageously funny things and to remember events as much nostalgic as utterly absurd. She brought up a particular memory that showcased her continuing obsession with Paco's infidelity. She directed herself to her sister Marina, and we were all listening:

Mercedes: Marina, remember when Paco was at the Embassy, and you [and Amado, her husband] came to visit us in Madrid, and Paco showed you around the Embassy? You were very impressed, weren't you?

Marina: Oh, yes. But those were sad times. Let's try not to remember them.

Mercedes: Oh, it was wonderful. All those parties, all those people, all those Americans, like me.

Miguel: Mom, you're not "all American," you're a naturalized citizen.

Mercedes: 100 percent. [When she spoke to English speakers she would often say, "I yam Amerreecan, hundre baee jundre." [r's rolling and guttural Spanish j sounds replacing the English h].

Marina: Yes, I remember you and Paco were pretty well-off.

Mercedes: By the way, Marina, remember when Paco, you, Amado, and some others were dining at that table, and you and Paco stepped out? [No reaction from Marina.] Don't you remember? [My mom looking accusingly straight into her sister's eyes.] Where did you and Paco go?

Marina's reaction was at first indignation, then disbelief at what my mother was suggesting. My aunt said, "But Mercedes, how in the world do you expect me to remember that?" And with that question we were all in stitches. All except my mom, whose tone as she asked the question had been perfectly serious. But mercifully, when she heard our collective laughter, she too cracked a smile.

Some say jealousy is a mark of self-loathing or lack of confidence. In the case of Mercedes, there certainly is something to that. She was the daughter of a writer, a man of the world, and she had not gotten very far in her own education. She had nothing to blame herself for—the obstacles to women's education, even those of the upper classes, were many. Perhaps more important, like with so many women regardless of the historical period or the culture, appearance is everything. And I suspect, actually now I know, she did not think she was beautiful. She hated her nose, the color of her hair, her legs, and her overall look. She thought she was fat. In the dementia years, when she had lost some forty or fifty pounds, she looked emaciated. But from her upper seventies to her death I saw in her eyes that she felt good about finally having lost what she thought was excess weight.

But I prefer another explanation of her jealousy. She just didn't trust my father, and perhaps in his comments or facial expressions he had given her reason not to trust him. Moreover, after the initial total attraction to Mercedes, he took up another love: his career. Indeed, when he became a professor of Spanish language, literature, and the humanities at Dartmouth, he discovered his true calling. He turned from Mercedes to Unamuno, Galdós, Azorín, St. Augustine, Plato, and many of the other greats. He passed all that on to me, and I'm grateful. But I sense now, as I have grown older than he, he could have opened his eyes a bit wider to take another look at Mercedes. But then again, I feel for him too—it's upsetting. He too felt inadequate in that elite academic atmosphere where most of his colleagues had PhDs from the most prestigious institutions in the U.S. Growing up, when all that superiority was said and done, I think both my mom and dad felt that in the long run they didn't belong.

Mercedes' years in Hanover as a faculty wife and mother at Dartmouth were, on the surface, happy ones. Compared to that previous life in the Old World, when she had to deal with the trials of her brother and father, when the bombs made it unsafe to walk in the streets of Madrid, compared to all that, the tranquility, natural beauty, innocence, acceptance, and everything that accompanied life in her New World, she was in something akin to paradise. I remember well what happened to her when she went back to Spain after she had forged a new existence and identity in New England: the memories came back. For my dad too. It's not that they didn't enjoy those summers and sabbatical-year trips back to their previous life, it's that the memories were fraught, maybe even more for my dad than for my mom. Throughout this time my dad had bouts of depression. And for my mom, my dad's sickness made her feel not only that something was terribly wrong, it was also a sign that she too was sick.

But let's turn this around. Paco's active libido was a concern of hers, yes, but what about *her* desires? I believe it has taken our cultures a long time, both the Spanish and the American, to come to terms with women's libido. I think of all those Douglas Sirk movies of the fifties, like *All That Heaven Allows*, and the brilliant 2002 homage film to Sirk by Todd Haynes, *Far from Heaven*, in which there is an adulterous relationship between a black man and a middle-class white woman. In Spain, the real social change after the death of Franco was in sexual mores—a new acknowledgment of women's sexuality. I remember that my mom, both before and after my dad died, had sexual fantasies concerning her doctors. I'll leave out the names, but when I was moving her out of her home in New Hampshire, I found letters from a Dr. X thanking her for her many letters in which she requested more information about her health along with a suggestion that they discuss it in the hospital cafeteria. I also remember that the name of this doctor would come up often, and my father's reaction was not as much jealous as embarrassment and criticism of his wife's view of reality; she was delusional.

As I think back on this, it occurs to me that maybe it would have been better for my father to show some jealousy, a recognition that Mercedes and he were both sexual beings, that love is complex, that desire will always be a reality, and perhaps most of all, that the "wind under his wings" when he set sail for the New World was a strikingly beautiful woman who was much more than just a faculty wife. I wish he would have been a bit more like Romeo and a little less like Paco.

Chapter Nine

Leaping into the Gorge

A Dartmouth College Professor of Spanish, Francisco Ugarte, committed suicide shortly before noon [yesterday] by leaping from the 100-yard-high Quechee Gorge Bridge.
(Special to the *New York Times*, September 6, 1969.)

This news clip could have continued with something like "Prior to September 5, 1969, Francisco's wife, Mercedes Precioso Ugarte, had led a relatively happy life with her husband and two children, George and Michael, in her newly adopted country. However, that happy life was shattered with a nervous breakdown when her second child was born, as well as a bout of tuberculosis about ten years later. Those who knew Professor Ugarte said he was distraught about his wife's illnesses." But the news media were not much interested in the details of this suicide, much less in the professor's life with Mercedes.

Despite her memories of difficult times in Spain as well as false (and maybe not-so-false) accusations of Paco's infidelity, Mercedes was enjoying a life of family harmony and, as she so desired, high status in the community. Her other desire was to feel safe, and she did; the paranoia had subsided. By 1969 there were no longer any enemies of the U.S. trying to do in her husband.

She did go back to Spain, but not because she had to—it was to accompany her husband and children. Yes, the trips back to that other life, seven of them from 1954 to 1969, were for her and were family fun-filled vacations like those of anyone visiting sunny Spain during the first tourist boom—except when they weren't. My dad's plan was to retire in Spain, a good move on his part, not only because of a deep wish (albeit conflicted) to return, but also because living in Spain at that time was a major bargain. And my father always watched his dollars and *pesetas* carefully. The powers that be at Dartmouth told him he had to publish if he wanted to remain at the College, so he went to work. As enterprising as he was, he worked at something that might yield some profit along with job security: textbooks. He published several of them, and they were remarkably successful. Of special interest to me were his texts on Spanish civilization. My mom liked them too—for her they were signs that she had married a writer, like her father.

With his first Spanish language textbook followed by several others, he was able to go back to Spain in style. Things were good for all of us, particularly my mom, who enjoyed the new house and all the things she could buy after living through wartime scarcity. But those trips back were not always blissful. In fact, things happened in Spain that made for a great deal of marital turmoil.

As a teenager the last thing I wanted to think about was the bickering between my mom and dad. At times I got drawn into the conflicts, usually siding with my father, but my hopes and concerns were at first those of a snotty-nosed preppy: sports, girls, my looks, and an occasional idea about the meaning of life, the Vietnam War, or the civil rights movement. I was closer to my dad than my mom, so I thought my mom was a woman not in the same league as someone with the expertise and education of my father. I sensed she cared more about Vietnam than the plight of African Americans, because of her direct wartime experience. The few political opinions my mom expressed were shared by those who shouted, "No more bombs!"

So why did she tell me I'd look great in uniform? This happened while driving back to my prep school. On the road at nighttime from Hanover to Plymouth, New Hampshire, my dad was driving—he hated driving, mostly because my mom would always tell him that he was going in the wrong direction. A back-seat driver she was not; she was more like a loud passenger-seat know-it-all with no idea where she was or how to get to the desired destination. She couldn't stop talking. And her mispronunciations of the destinations made it worse: Durham was Dudam, Hanover was Janover—

with that hard Spanish j sound—New Hampshire was *Niu-Hamsheer*, Cleveland, where my dad occasionally taught in summer school, had three syllables, *Clee-va-lan*, Chicago was *Chee-ca-go*, and later when she spoke to my son-in-law who lived there, she would say *Sheet-ca-go*, and they would both laugh heartily. For this I tended to defend my dad; after all, he was the one with a formal education. But this night I lost it. As we talked about my life at the prep school, she suggested it would be so perfectly nice if the school had an ROTC program—which it didn't—and that I should think about getting into it because I would look dashing in a military uniform.

Ay Ay Ay. I went crazy. With the Ugartes, the conflicts were never violent, they were always verbal and histrionic. "*Pero Mamá, ¿qué diablos dices?*" (Mother, what the hell are you saying?), or I might have said, "*¿Qué coño dices?*" ("coño" refers to female anatomy) literally What in the world of cunts are you saying?), and I went on half in Spanish, one fourth in English, and the last fourth in grunts, groans, dramatic noises, and curses in a language I like to call the Esperanto of anger. When she said, "*Pero qué guapo vestido de marinero, como los Kennedy*" (How handsome in a sailor's suit, like the Kennedys); it was a confirmation that my mom had no idea who I was or what my inclinations were. I was forging an identity, and she was not only ignorant of it, she thought she could create one for me. Bad mothering? Half a century later, I think that explanation needs some editing. Despite her genuine abhorrence of war, my mother needed positive images and stories, romantic narratives of dashing young men, often in sparkling military uniforms, who catch the eyes of pretty women related to powerful men, like Joe Kennedy Jr. when he was in the Navy after his visit to the U.S. Embassy. There were also family pictures of her brother-in-law in his Republican military uniform, even a photo of her brother as a young handsome man in uniform; that he was a Communist was of no consequence as long as he looked good in a military suit. She wanted at least one of her sons to follow in their footsteps. But all this, as I look back at it, had less to do with reality than with stories, fictions she projected onto her own life.

My dad tried to correct her pronunciation as well as her perception of her children, showing his superiority, informing her that Miguel didn't want any part of the military, to which my mother would lash out at him, telling him to keep his eyes on the road, as in "Never mind, *si tú no sabes nada de nada*" (you know nothing about nothing). She just knew, she desired, that at least one of her sons would show off his good looks by wearing a dressy uniform—besides, she still thought I was blond, which was not true. Whatever "good" she thought these young soldiers were doing in the military was far less important than their relationships with the women who had fallen for them. These kinds of arguments that often included my brother, who had the good sense to stay away from the family as much as he could, were much too frequent. And it seemed to me that the longer Paco and Mercedes were together, the more intense the animosity became. What I did not realize then is that they both were sick (in the head).

The squabbles were more intense when they were in Spain. As I try to make sense of those trips back to where they were reared, where they fell in love and married, where they had their first child, and where they both thrived and suffered, my sense is that their success in the New World was never something that went unqualified. My parents loved going back, and they hated it. But they both loved and hated it in different ways. I vaguely remember their first trip back, which was also my first taste of a geography totally unfamiliar to me at age five.

The year was 1954. The Ugarte-Precioso family had arrived by means of the same transportation that had taken them away: an ocean liner. This one, the *Queen Mary*, docked at Le Havre, France, after the voyage from New York. In those days it was cheaper to travel overseas by ship than by plane. For me, that trip had something of a surreal quality, not only because I barely remember it, but because it seemed I had entered a new planet. Upon our arrival, my dad had rented a car to travel from Le Havre to Paris. From there to Madrid by train and from Madrid to Hellín by another rented car. Part of the road to Hellín was not paved. Given my dad's loathing for four-wheel vehicles, also that we were arriving to our destination after night had fallen, and that my mom was so high-strung, my dad was utterly exhausted, although he was still young, only forty-five.

But when we finally got there, we entered a beautiful palatial home of two stories just across the street from the Hellín bullring. There was a winding staircase leading to the upstairs and a chandelier that reminded me of a Disney movie. My aunt's husband, Amado, and some of his family members had done very well as owners of a wheat processing factory, selling flour to bakeries all over Spain. The factory was part of the estate. The entire complex had a wonderful name: La Gracia (Grace). And when we got there after that seemingly endless journey—both away from home and back home—I remember everyone, especially my mom as she covered her face and wept. Hugs, kisses, touching, followed by more hugs, kisses, and touching. It was the emigrant-exile's return, the archetypal moment of arrival—even if it was not to the home she grew up in—almost too much for her to bear. My dad was not as emotional, but he remembered, nostalgically and painfully, the good times and bad times in his life.

Both my mom and dad were happy to see everyone, not only on this first trip, but on all the others that followed. They were even more happy to tell them how well they had done in that little town in New Hampshire in all its greenery—a stark contrast to the environs of Hellín. My dad described our new residence and let on about how successful he had been as a professor of Spanish at a fancy college, how my mother was so admired by the other faculty wives because she spoke French and was learning English. She too would rant on about the parties ("pawtees") she threw for the French speakers among the women connected to Dartmouth, since no one spoke Spanish. None of her family members knew what "pawtees" were, but they figured it out.

Their two most prized trophies were their children: Jorge—then age ten, a handsome boy, a bit on the dark side, well-rounded physically and personally—and little Miguel age five, blond at that time, not quite as smiley as his older brother, and quieter. Both of us spoke Spanish, but I used lots of English words, more so than my brother. That made my mom grin, she too would insert a couple of English expressions and place names into her speech with more than a little affectation, as in "Okaaiii," "Daaaarmuth," "pawty," "sangweech," "jot (hot) dog" (j is guttural), "meelk" (two syllables). My father was equally boastful but in a different way. He had accomplished things in the land of opportunity. As he looked around his old country, he didn't like what he saw, and at every opportunity, he would tell his family and friends that the U.S. was the land of the future and Spain was backward, full of dust and patronage, and of course nothing worked. "The most frequent sign I see around here is '*No Funciona*' (Out of Order)." I'm not sure my mother agreed, since there was always a subaltern around to fix it. As long as her family knew they had high status in their adopted land, she was fine. Keeping up appearances, regardless of the inner hardship: that's what Mercedes was interested in during these trips back home to the family.

But we did not only go back to Hellín; we took advantage of what the Spanish coastline had to offer. Spain is a peninsula with a coastline of some three thousand miles on the Mediterranean and the Atlantic, so after the war, the economic opportunities related to tourism were seemingly endless, not only for hotels and resorts, but for everything related: construction, restaurants, cafés, nightclubs, museums, tours, study abroad programs. My dad saw this and took advantage, more from the consumer end than the vendor since the *peseta* was so cheap. And he had the added advantage of having family in various parts of Spain. His brother—remember Javier, the Anglophile?—married a woman from Barcelona whose son (Javierito) discovered a picturesque, sunny little town on the Costa Brava a few miles south of the French border: San Miguel de Colera, or just Colera.

Javierito had been successful at renting camping spots to French, British, German, and other European tourists. Because my Tío Javier was close to my father, his son Javierito invited us to Barcelona and then to a little beach town. The pebble beach of Colera, its coves filled with shellfish of all varieties, had waters as pure and transparent as those of the Caribbean. Both my mom and dad loved it there, more so my dad, since he was from the north. As a professor of language and language proficient in his own right, he enjoyed practicing the Catalan he knew, something that eventually rubbed off on me. The Ugartes of the Basque country, the next generation of which was all Catalan-speaking due to Uncle Javier's move, loved this about my dad as did the many friends Paco and Mercedes made. Not as much my mom, pure Manchega—not convinced that Catalan was a real language like French, she stuck to her Castilian with inflections of the Spanish spoken by the characters in *Don Quijote*. But people we associated with in that tiny Mediterranean beach town of less than a thousand souls seemed to like Paco, Merche, and their two boys. Looking back on those summers in Colera, it's hard not to feel that glint of nostalgia. Although we all need to be careful about our assessments of the past, today I want to convince myself that my memories of Colera are real. Those were pleasant days, although short-lived, not idyllic, agreeable, and I'd like to think that Paco and Mercedes thought so too.

That was the pattern of those trips back. The behavior of my parents was almost a caricature of returning emigrants from the Americas—the Spanish word is "indianos," proud, lots of money to throw around because things were cheap in the area to which they had returned. My father reinforced that common Spanish stereotype: "The U.S. is a great place to make money, and Spain the ideal place to spend it." Yes, it was embarrassing to me that in subsequent trips my dad ostentatiously transported his 1950-something gray Chevy across the Atlantic for all the poor Spanish souls to see. But make no mistake: both my mom and dad appreciated and loved the human contact and warmth that they did not find in frigid New Hampshire, as well as the food. Imagine what this couple had to eat in New Hampshire in the fifties; just look at one episode of *Mad Men*: lots of pre-prepared dinners with spongy Bimbo bread. My mom learned to cook in the States, because as a child and young woman, all that domestic activity had been taken care of by servants. My mom saw the convenience foods of the U.S. in the fifties as a wonderful advancement especially appropriate to a woman like her, who'd had other women do the cooking.

But U.S. fifties food was not to her Paco's liking; not only was it something he would never become used to, he loathed it. Less so my mom; this was one of the many traits that set her apart from the typical Spanish *ama de casa* (housewife), if there is such a thing: she did not express a great deal of interest in food. She had no idea what she was doing in the kitchen at first, and when she got the hang of it, she blessed us with hot dogs, peanut butter sandwiches, and an occasional roast chicken with mashed potatoes and overly cooked green beans for Sunday dinner in the early afternoon, Spanish hours. I was okay with that; not sure about my brother, typical teenager, always looking for ways to stay away from the family; Paco, on the other hand, despite the pleasantness of the situation and the surroundings, suffered, both in spirit and in his heart-felt (and palette-felt) critiques of U.S. fifties cuisine, a kind of suffering directly attributed to his illness.

One of the contributing factors to my father's growing depression was the food he had to eat in his new (otherwise wonderful) country; he told me so. It was also an indirect cause of his marital dissatisfaction; if Merche could not give him intellectual stimulation, the least she could do was try to cook Spanish-style, but no. Of course, there were other causes. For the

Ugarte family, speculation on the causes of my dad's illness and eventual suicide is endless: chemical imbalance, his father's neglect, Spain's dictatorial tendencies, his pride, his own sense of intellectual insecurity amidst all that Ivy-League pretension, and of course his wife. But of equal concern to me is to figure out how his mental illness affected Mercedes. For my mom, Paco's depression was utterly incomprehensible. Although she never articulated how she felt, I suspect she may have blamed herself. What I do know is that she yelled at him a lot; understandable to me today, because my father was so critical of her. But when he was feeling deeply depressed, sometimes he stopped talking. I remember one time in Hanover when we expressed excitement about a coming summer trip to Spain, he just sat down and sobbed, much to my mother's amazement and chagrin, because she had no access into his dark world; none of us did. As a matter of fact, when he got into his at times paralyzing melancholia, she did not sympathize. Just the opposite—she yelled at him. "*Paco, levántate, por dios, que son las doce* (Paco, get out of bed for god's sake, it's twelve o'clock).

But his world was not the only one that got dark. My mom's did too every now and then, and sometimes she threw us all for a loop. Those dark periods seemed to get their darkest when she was in Spain. One day when we were in Hellín, and my dad was on a sabbatical leave, my mom had what my family called an *ataque de nervios*, a general term referring to an "attack" of something in the body or in the head that throws you out of kilter, like panic or high anxiety. I remember it as if it might have been a dream, a bad one. I was only ten. She yelled at her sister, her eyes opened widely, her arms and hands flailing, "*Marina, nos vamos a un hotel*" (Marina, we're going to a hotel). I saw my dad looking at her as if he was ashamed, utterly disgusted by her behavior and words. His sympathy lay elsewhere. I don't think I ever heard him try to explain to me or to anyone what could possibly lead my mom into such a state. I recall it was after a scrumptious mid-day dinner my aunt Marina had planned and her servants had prepared. Mom claimed she was upset because she thought we were overstaying our welcome in the Giménez-Precioso household. But to this day I do not know for sure what triggered the attack. Indeed we stayed there for what I remember to be a long time, over several months. My dad was tired of staying there too.

My mom suffered consistently from *ataques de nervios*, like the one that began my life in 1949. *Histérica.* That was my dad's explanation. Feminists have cautioned us about that word, its gender bias, and the plethora of psychological and psychiatric theories surrounding hysteria and histrionics. Whatever our conclusions about the reality or falseness of that word, I can attest that my mom fit the bill. She was at times a true hysteric, and she let the world know it. When I think of Bertha in *Jane Eyre* and its sequel *Wide Sargasso Sea* (written well after Charlotte Bronte's famous novel), I think of the ways my mom acted out the role of Bertha, the madwoman in the attic, the one who lives as a constant reminder to her "keepers" (or jailers) of the ways she's been mistreated. As readers we suspect that the attic is the only place Bertha is free to be herself. God help us if she breaks out. Mercifully, unlike Bertha, my mom managed to keep herself from burning down the house. But like Bertha, Mercedes' weirdness had its own story—before she crossed another sea.

The year my mom displayed that memorable family outburst was the year my parents decided to send my brother and me to a boarding school run by Marist brothers in Murcia, about an hour away from Hellín. What in God's name were my parents thinking? A little boy, and his older brother with problems of his own, had to deal every day with the worst of Spanish traditionalism—from educational practices to religious indoctrination—and a Spanish Catholic ideology (remember the Inquisition?) that neither of my parents agreed with. And when they came to visit me, what did my mom feel when she had to say goodbye until next week to a weeping boy of ten and his brother of fifteen? She must have wept too; I'd like to think that's true. Clearly, we were strangers in that school, outsiders in every sense, and my mom and dad knew it. I got into fights defending I'm not sure what—my identity? They called me "the Yankee," the Spanish term for "gringo." And no matter how much the Marist brothers tried to protect me, I ended up not trusting them. I was never molested, but I suspect some of the boys were. What I do remember are the beatings; again, I was not a victim, even though I was just as mischievous as the ones who were slapped around—an advantage of being a Yankee. I didn't know it at the time, but they were intimidated by my presence.

None of the boys had much affection for these celibate religious men; they had names for them, like *El Hermano Girafa* (Brother Giraffe) named for his long neck, and *Foca* (Seal) because of his nervous twitch: two Spanish Mr. Choakumchilds, right out of Dickens' *Hard Times*, or better yet, right out of my grandfather's autobiographical writing. I vaguely remember telling my mom about Brother Rafael, a mystic, who would walk up and down the rows of beds in our huge sleeping quarters amidst a darkness so black that I could not believe how he didn't stumble. The soles of his shoes were hard, and as he walked over the hard surface, the sound of his stride—clop, clop, clop—got more intense the closer he got to my bed, and less so as he passed by.

My mom's complicity in the decision to send us to this awful school is unclear to me. My dad's reason was that he wanted us to learn Castilian Spanish so that we would never forget. It worked.

There was one last trip to Spain in the summer of 1969. Two or three years prior, my father had bought the condominium on the Mediterranean in a beach area about ten miles north of Alicante city. It was our refuge, our "castle in Spain," as my brother used to call it, with its ideal location overlooking the beach and its three bedrooms, much larger than those of normal Spanish apartments. Small groceries, bakeries, and cafés had begun to sprout up nearby with the rise of Spain's tourist industry. We loved it—the beach, the food, the relaxed summer atmosphere, the sun, the kinship, at once with real kin as well as with friends old and new. In some ways, we too were tourists, my mom and dad outsiders visiting in their own land. My father was conflicted about feeling that way, my mom less so. She liked her new role as an outsider.

My mother and father decided to make that trip to Alicante—they didn't know it would be the last one for my dad. I have vague recollections of the pre-trip preparation. My dad was more excited about it than usual, and my mom seemed to be keeping him in line, making sure he didn't go overboard. As I look back on that time, my sense is that he was in a manic stage. And Mercedes was suffering from his suffering, although she didn't know how to put words to that experience, just dramatic protests that my father was behaving badly. That was when he said he wanted to go to the San Fermín festival in Pamplona to run in front of the bulls at age fifty-nine imitating Hemingway. "*Pero Paco, ¿Adónde quieres ir? ¿A Pamplona? ¡Pero tú estás loco!*

Yo no voy." (But Paco, where do you want to go? Pamplona? You're crazy! I'm not going). Bipolar was a term that came later; the designation in his day was "manic-depressive psychosis." I recall his psychiatrist using that term when I went to see him shortly after my father's death. My question today is, how do family members cope with a loved one who announces wild plans and goes into a rage when someone tells him the plans are *crazy?* The question is more urgent if the loved one is a spouse or lover. My recollection of this scene got worse when my aunt Marina told me that her daughter saw Paco exposing himself to her, and he wasn't in a dressing room or on the beach drying himself. My memory of that month before my dad threw himself off the gorge remains a memory of others as well as my own fraught recollection, so all I can do now is imagine, and my imaginings are disturbing.

I went to Alicante on my own that summer to join them. It was the summer of two monumental happenings in U.S. and world history—the moon landing and Edward Kennedy's Chappaquiddick transgression (or crime?) causing the death of Mary Jo Kopechne. To add to that, there was the private incident—in the Ugarte-Precioso family that same summer: the suicide of Francisco Ugarte Cristóbal.

There was not enough time for me to travel with Paco and Mercedes on their summer trip to Spain. I had activities of my own, so I decided to join them in late July of 1969; they had been there since early June. I was a young adult of twenty. When I arrived a month before their scheduled return to Dartmouth for the fall term, my dad was delighted to see me, more than usual. I found him extremely excitable, and Mom couldn't relax because Dad couldn't relax. When I arrived my mom immediately described the details of my father's extreme behavior. My reaction was to tell them both that they should get a divorce. I had just received a rather severe battery of women's liberation from several of my female college friends, and as a consequence I had begun to see my parents' relationship as the manifestation of male hierarchy. I self-righteously and condescendingly explained all this to them as if I had all the experience in the world, an adolescent-young man with the weight of society on his shoulders. I sensed that my dad was taking me more seriously than my mother, who was the one who should have thought more about it. But, after all, she thought, what does your second-born son know of your travails?

A few months later, after the tragedy, I remember Mercedes telling me that my father had been writing in a diary before I arrived, and that at one point he decided to burn its pages. I have no idea what was in them, although I have often speculated. Were they a long, drawn-out suicide note? Were they notes describing his mental anguish and despair? I returned to the States and tried not to think of the snake pit they had created out of a sunny seaside apartment with a balcony overlooking the body of water that remains a heaven of relaxation and pleasure, not only for outsiders, but also for all those expat Brits escaping the incessant clouds of their daily lives—Spaniards too, lots of them from Madrid, Murcia, and Albacete.

I remember a specific evening with invited guests on that very balcony when U.S. astronauts had reached the moon. "*Don Francisco, hemos llegado a la luna*" (Francisco, we have arrived on the moon), said one of our visitors, a pedantic professor at the University of Murcia, who tried to utter that phrase in Latin, as if to inform us that we humans are all connected. I thought he was a bore at the time, but now I think he was right—to say this in Latin was a great rejoinder to Neil Armstrong's "One small step . . ." My father responded by going into a pedantic rant of his own about God knows what. My mother conversed with the pedant's non-Latin-speaking wife, a very proper woman nonetheless, whom my mom thought was worse than stodgy, a *beata* (pious woman), always referencing the Good Lord or the Virgin Mary. Man to man, woman to woman, that was the pattern; they rarely crossed that gender divide when they socialized. After that visit, I was looking forward to going back to the familiar confines of New Hampshire. What my mom was thinking at this time I can only surmise: she was deeply worried about Paco; she had no idea what was afflicting him, much less the causes, although she ventured explanations in her own mind.

Years later when I tried (unsuccessfully, perhaps cruelly) to get her to confront her past, she told me, as she had before, that her husband could not have killed himself. "*No. Eso es imposible. ¿Tú de verdad crees que se mató?*" (No. That's impossible. Do you really think he killed himself?). I answered, "Yes. He was sick." She could not wrap her mind around that notion of infirmity. Sickness is when you have the flu, or TB, or cancer. This was the early 70s; knowledge of my dad's type of illness, especially among people of my mom's generation, was not common.

Later she told me about their trip back just a few days before my father's final act. They stayed at a hotel in New York, where my mother ordered bacon and eggs for breakfast; she was hungry after the flight from Madrid. My dad said he didn't want anything. But when the waiter brought my mom her food, he suddenly changed his mind. Mercedes told me he inched his fork closer to her plate and asked sheepishly if he could have a bite, but she pulled her plate back. She told me about this a few months after the tragedy. My mother and I were talking about my dad as we rode a bus from Boston to Hanover after she had gone to visit my brother and his family. It was nighttime, and she was telling me she did not have the generosity to give my hungry father a half strip of bacon the morning after their flight. "How could you?" I asked. She didn't reply. I was becoming unhinged. "Why did you do that?" I don't remember if other passengers on the bus heard me; my voice was getting loud, my tone exasperated. She answered, "*Pues, pa fastidiarle*" (Well, to annoy him).

It sounded to me like she didn't care that she had hurt him, or that she was putting salt in his excruciatingly painful wounds. At that time I considered it torture. I'm not proud to say that I "lost it." I called her a cruel woman, a bitch, and God knows what else. My words to her on that bus were beneath me and beneath us all, but those words were natural in the Ugarte-Precioso family squabbles. It was our custom that an affront to someone's pride would be answered by the most insulting words imaginable. Pain. Drama. Anguish. My mom was the queen of all that and an unwitting teacher. The more drama the better for everybody, because when it's over there is tremendous relief. This time, however, there was no relief. Her words and mine have taken up permanent residency in my head, and not as something that leads to peace of mind.

In Hanover on that fateful day of September 5, 1969, my dad was still in bed at nine thirty or so, which was not his custom; he was an early riser, and on this he prided himself. When it was a nice day he would look around at the lilacs, pines, elms, and the white birches of New Hampshire, at the clouds and the sky, and say "*¡Qué día!*" (What a [beautiful] day!). But not on the morning of September 5. I remember it was a nice day, but the darkness in his mind had taken over. He remained in bed after my mom had gotten up to clean and rearrange household things after an absence of several months.

I caught a glimpse of him lying in his bedroom as I went downstairs; he was on his back staring upward, his nose pointing at the ceiling, his eyes squinting. *¡Qué día!* was not in his parlance or consciousness that day. I had gone into the backyard, and suddenly he emerged from the kitchen door leading out to the yard; he walked over to me deliberately, and said something I'll never forget: "*Tu madre me está haciendo la vida imposible*" (Your mother is making my life impossible). I looked away in disgust, as if to say, "Don't tell me about your problems. Get over it."

Several hours later, when I was with my friend Dennis watching Hanover High School football or soccer practice, I saw my old coach approaching me accompanied by a policeman. I intuited what was wrong, for some reason I can't figure out my own intuition. I thought at that moment he had tried to do something to himself, and sure enough, it was not that he was in jail for reckless driving. I was right; he had killed himself. I felt a split second of shock, despair, denial all at once. But almost immediately my thoughts turned to Mercedes. How could she possibly deal with this? This was the beginning of the end for her. I went back home and saw she was talking to a policeman and a priest. She was numb, expressionless, oblivious to what was happening. Later a doctor came to our house to give her a sedative—a needle, not a pill. For the next day or so, she was almost comatose, under the influence of God knows what drug, looking into space as if she had left her own body. Memories of Brattleboro.

Did I say almost comatose? No. Comatose. Zombie-like for the next few weeks in which all the details of a death in the family had to be taken care of: informing family and friends, doctors, funeral arrangements, burial, lawyers, my brother's trip to New Hampshire from Los Angeles, receiving all the neighbors, colleagues, and faculty wives expressing condolences. My brother and I answered with gratitude for the sentiments and all the food they had brought, all that death-cake. I remember a couple of the faculty wives asking me about my mother. I told them the facts, no analysis or opinion or feeling. I remember their expressions of pathos. My mother would not have liked this: humiliation on top of devastation.

At the funeral my mom was still in a state of semi-consciousness. She approached the corpse as I imagined she had done just after her mother died when she was a little girl of five. But this time, a woman of fifty-six, she was anything but pathetically innocent. Pathetic, yes, but now in a bad way. She had lived a life of relative joy and fulfillment, interrupted by episodes of turmoil so intense that they took back from the joy and fulfillment in the New World. All that time she knew about falseness and deceit, or she thought she knew, because she often invented those things when there was no reason. And this would turn out to be the most monumental falseness of her life. That was not her husband lying there in a suit he barely ever wore, his neck puffed out, eyes closed as if he were asleep, hands folded across his waist, that Ugarte nose, pointing upward, as if he were in bed next to her. *They've done an acceptable job in replicating him, but they don't fool me*, she thought. *Paco has fled. I don't know where he is, but I'll find him.*

Weeks later, she snapped out of that suspicion. The thoughts about Paco's abandonment were fleeting; she let us know, albeit deceptively, that she would be all right in the long run. Years later (fifty of them), I came upon a letter she had written to the family in Spain about three weeks after it happened. It was to the Ugartes who had moved to Barcelona. Here is my translation:

> *Los Angeles 10/23/69*
> *Dear Javier and Elvirita:*
> *We received Javierito's letter that Miguel sent me.* [Remember, Javierito is my dad's brother's son, but I don't recall that letter. I too was in my own state of denial]. *A week after my beloved poor Paco died, I went to Los Angeles with Jorge* [my brother George]. *Jorge and his wife came to Hanover; they would not allow me to stay there [alone] under any circumstances. So just a week after Paco died, I found myself in Los Angeles where my grandchildren kept me from succumbing. My life has ended. I can't live without him.*
>
> *Here I have a two-door, six-cylinder car so I can drive little Andrew to daycare and go shopping in Los Angeles. My grandchildren are very smart and good looking.*
>
> *I'll go to Hanover around the beginning of November. Jorge wants us all to live here. Miguel can transfer to a university [in LA]. Here it's always summer.*

> I agree with Javier that Paco could not have committed suicide; it was probably an accident.
>
> We arrived at Hanover on Thursday the 4th, in the afternoon. On Friday the 5th, in the morning, Paco got up late. He did not say a word; he got in the car even though there was something wrong with it, so Miguel and I thought he had taken it to the shop. That was around twelve, and at four a policeman came to tell me the incredible news, that he had jumped off a hundred-meter bridge. Paco was depressed after Miguel left Alicante. He did not want to write you; he seemed obsessed by something. We spent the night in New York, but he didn't want to stay there. The next day we went to Hanover by bus and Michael picked us up; he told us something was wrong with the car and we had to take it to be fixed, and that's where I thought he had gone. My sadness and horror is that I should have told him something, but he was set on not speaking. I don't know how to deal with so much pain.
>
> Your afflicted and disconsolate sister and aunt sends you all her love,
>
> Mercedes

Clearly Memory has let me down . . . or Memory let my mother down. Didn't I drive to Boston to pick them up? Maybe not; maybe I only drove to the bus station. Does it matter? Yes, because the picture my mom paints of herself is not exactly the one I am painting of her here, or the one I remember. This is a letter that Luis, Javierito's son-in-law, showed me as part of a family history he was compiling on the Ugartes. While Javierito is the one who wrote to my mom, my mother replies to his mother and father—Javier and Elvirita. This letter is the last they heard from us until about forty or so years later. I read these words as something like my mother's last gasp. She would not return to Spain until 1974, and this was largely at my urging, but she did not go north to see the Ugartes of Barcelona and Colera. Not once from that summer of 1969 to her death. Her place in post-Paco Spain was Alicante.

The letter is almost as painful to read today as it must have been for my mother to write. It reminds me of a Mercedes who could be remarkably lucid when she needed to be, willing to look at things head-on, honest, even earnest. It reminds me of the words she used in the Brattleboro mental record, trying to convince the medical personnel that she was okay. Yet the Mercedes who wrote those words is unrecognizable to the people who knew her well after her husband killed himself. It's understandable that she didn't accept that he killed himself. That's how many people deal initially with a suicide. However, to believe, as she did when she got back to Hanover from Los Angeles, that he was still alive is another matter. In fact she went looking for him. Yes, she had gone door to door in the neighborhood asking for Paco, also she had phoned people whom she thought might know where he was. Here was a woman looking for her dead husband. That corpse buried in the Pine Knoll Cemetery was not him.

Many years later, my mother, brother, and I were in the office of a public notary in Alicante who was helping us with the labyrinthine paperwork to transfer the Alicante property ownership from my father to his heirs. He never wrote a will. We were very close to resolving complicated legal problems surrounding the inheritance, when my mother, who had been uncharacteristically silent, blurted out in the middle of something the agent was trying to explain, "And what if he's still alive?" The agent stopped in mid-sentence, eyes wide open, looking directly at my mother. I remember she was smiling coyly as both Jorge and Miguel blurted out in unison and almost as dramatically as she, "No, no no! He's been dead for decades. You have the death certificate."

How I remember that mischievous smile. Calling attention to herself was a game she played to win, and she was almost always victorious. But it was more than that. From September 5, 1969, to her death, she entertained the idea that Paco had abandoned her—in the physical sense of taking a trip or getting the hell out of there. At first this idea of hers was a real one, a true belief, and convincing her otherwise was nearly impossible. Then gradually it turned into a metaphor, as in, "He left me emotionally," to which she could have added, "for another woman." Paco's *departure* in the physical sense was another manifestation of her mantra: "Could be true and not have happened." And she was absolutely right. In the long run, she was right. He did just as she thought: he abandoned her and his family.

But at this point in my life, well after her death, I think of her as a survivor. She had lived through her mom's death at age five, the Spanish Civil War, her father's death sentence and incarceration, and now this. She survived by inventing realities and by often uttering another of her pat phrases:

"Eess good to be alieeve"; the second vowel of "alive" sounded like ay. And alive she was. Paco be damned, wherever he was.

Paco and Mercedes at gathering in Bema, Dartmouth College; circa 1956

Mercedes in the backyard of apartment building on Park Street in Hanover, N.H.
The gray Chevy was their first car; circa 1953

The Ugartes the year I was born
Hanover, New Hampshire, 1949

Mercedes teaching a class of Spanish conversation to Dartmouth College students
circa 1950

The Ugartes
2 Dana Drive. Hanover, New Hampshire
circa 1957

Mercedes Skiing Dartmouth Golf Course
circa 1956

Francisco, Mercedes, George
and Michael Ugarte

Ugarte Christmas card
circa 1958

Michael (the author) at the top of Cerro del Pino overlooking the town where both Mercedes and Paco were born. Hellin, Spain 1955

That's me on the burro in front of the buildling where Mercedes' father had spent his final years under house arrest. Isso, Spain 1955

Back patio of my Aunt Marina and Uncle Amado's dwelling they called "La Gracia" My mom is next to me; I'm the last one on the right in the back row. Hellin, Spain; circa 1965

Part IV

Chapter Ten

One Hundred Years of Solitude

Why doesn't Mercedes comb her hair? Why doesn't grandma wear the nice sweater we got her for Christmas? Why is that chair on top of the sofa? Does my mom get enough to eat? Does Mercedes see any of her old friends? Why is Mercedes mean to the guy who's trying to fix her plumbing? Why does your mother say those things? Is she crazy? What does she mean? Mercedes, *¡Qué pelos! ¿Es que no vas a la peluquería?* (Mercedes, your hair! Don't you go to a hair dresser?) Answer to all the above: one hundred years of solitude.

The person asking my mom that last question was her sister Marina well after Paco's tragedy, and it is her sister Marina who answered it for her. After September 5, 1969, my mother's life changed drastically; nothing would be the same, no matter how much she wanted to bring that previous life back, no matter how determined she was, how steadfastly she insisted that her husband, Paco, her boyfriend-uncle of whom her father had not approved, her companion, her rival, her provider, her nemesis, her pain in the ass, her lover, the one who kissed her ever-so-chastely acting in a scene of *Romeo and Juliet*, the one with whom she'd had two beautiful boys, the one who wouldn't stop talking, the one who fled to who knows where with who knows who, that man, Paco, was absent from then on. Sure, he could have run off to Boston, or California, or Hellín, or Bilbao, or Rio de Janeiro, but the undeniable reality is that he was no longer around—the one who defined who she was. Now it would be one hundred years of no Paco.

Solitude yes, but ill fortune no. My dad had always been a good provider, and the success of his textbooks added a cushion to my mom's widow's pension. Thanks to my brother's financial know-how and a wonderful bank administrator, Mr. Gamble, Mercedes was left well-off in her abandonment. Her financial well-being was never an issue, unless one suspects that she used it not to buy herself extravagant things, but to keep in touch with family members who needed her generosity, and she was generous to a fault. She should have bought herself things to keep up her appearance, but she gradually let herself go.

The reality of those hundred years of solitude in Hanover, thirty of them in real time, is difficult to describe; in fact it's impossible because my mother's reality is always elusive. She herself sought to remember those years by attempting to write a book—*Los años después* (*The Years After*)—a few notebooks of which are in my possession. But those notebooks do not get at the reality of Mercedes. I can see that she tried, but I'm a bit disappointed at the result: though she was attuned to the power of words and cadences, her narrative renderings of situations are taken from *novelas rosas* (romantic novelettes), the kind her father had conceived and published with such success. But, much unlike my grandfather, she paid no attention to moving along a plot. Also disappointing is that she rarely speaks in her writing of the traumatic things that happened to her throughout her life. It seems Mercedes could not dwell on the tragic because it was too much, it was excessive, and if she "went there," if she faced her tragedy head-on, she would never return.

Looking at the events as I remember them, starting from her coming back home from LA to her definitive departure from Hanover thirty years later, I see a jumble of experiences, all in a haze that fuses the dryness and bougainvillea-filled seaside of Alicante with the lushness of New Hampshire—and my mother in between. During those years my mom got older, from a fifty-six-year-old woman, still pretty, still coquettish, to a weird old lady whose coquettishness was a marker of who she was, even though it had become somewhat grotesque as she aged. I was also evolving from a spoiled brat with intellectual revolutionary pretentions into an overly responsible career-minded *paterfamilias*. From the day of the tragedy on, my mom would turn into a thorn in my side.

In my second year of study at the University of New Hampshire, when I was visiting my mom, my father's psychiatrist summoned me to his office in Hanover for a chat. He told me he was concerned about my mother, that she was delusional, that for her own safety she should spend time at the mental health center at the Dartmouth Hitchcock Hospital. But there was a problem, because mental health professionals had begun to change their policy regarding commitment to mental treatment facilities. It became more and more difficult to commit a patient to an institution without their consent. It was up to me, said the good doctor, to convince my mom to sign a form that would allow the people in charge to take her away. Needless to say I was skeptical, but at age twenty, I was also clueless. I did as the professional said: I convinced my mom to sign a form. To this day I'm not sure what either of us thought she was signing. I barely recall the conversation. But I do know that she allowed the medical personnel to take her to the Hitchcock mental health facility where she stayed for a little over a month. I went back to school, and from there I called my brother and told him what was happening. He seemed to support my (and her?) decision. It goes against my inclinations to say, in light of all my skepticism about hospitals, institutions, and Michel Foucault's panopticon, that my mom's stay at this facility was positive. I looked all around for a piece of artwork she created while she was there. I found it some twenty years later and asked her about it. She gave it to me. It's a bronze engraving of a ballerina, a curved body seeming to fly through a gold metal background, arms reaching above her head. I have no idea how my mom made this, but I have always thought it touchingly beautiful, an image of what my mom (perhaps) wished she could be. In any case, she got better. The search for my dad subsided, she didn't make crazy phone calls any more, she stopped leaving her house to go door-to-door looking for Paco. I came back to Hanover from the university at least once a month and convinced myself that she was doing fine.

Thus began the next phase of her life—alone, resigned to an existence without Paco, constantly mindful of the lives of her two "boys," occasionally visiting or receiving old friends from town who had known her husband. My dad's colleague in Romance Languages at Dartmouth, Bob Russell, and his wife, June, did what they could to keep my mother in sync. A receptionist's job opened at one of the Johns Hopkins Center's art galleries on Wheelock Street in Hanover, about a twenty-minute walk from our house. "The Hop," as we called it, was a huge structure overlooking the campus green. It served as a center of culture of all sorts, with not only art exhibits, but theater, film, music, and an ample lounge on the second floor with a magnificent fireplace and an occasional piano player. The entire Ugarte family frequented it, and about a year after the tragedy it became a place of employment for my mom. Her job consisted of counting the number of people who came in to see an exhibit, and as she did so, she would look the part, play the role of a faculty wife who spoke English with an exotic accent, although Spanish was no longer as exotic a language as it was when she first arrived to Hanover. "Velcom. Ar ju heer for veeseet?" She would eye some of the pretty young women visitors, speculating that if they were a "dotter of a dotor [doctor]," they would be an excellent candidate for a date with her Maicol. She could not have been better at exuding Old-World charm.

These were not all bad years for Mercedes. I believe she liked the contact with people, as well as her workplace. For me it was an unexpected relief that she was working, receiving a wage, however minimal it was. When she wasn't at the gallery—it wasn't a daily job—she went to the movies occasionally, always walking, nearly always alone. In fact, I can't remember a single time she went to an event at The Hop with a companion, other than her visiting son. Indeed this was solitude, but not necessarily in the alienating sense. Her life had changed from identification with her husband to identification with her sons, and perhaps learning to identify with herself.

But that changed. After a five-year hiatus, we decided to go back to Spain for a summer visit, the first time without Paco, Mercedes the widow, and Miguel with a wife and her little grandson—age three—Francisco. What was disheartening about that first trip after Paco's demise, as I look back at it today, is that despite its overall positive effect, when we returned, no one did anything to renew Mercedes' arrangement as a receptionist at the art gallery. Many say we must live life without regrets. Who are they kidding? I regret many of my actions and attitudes toward my mother. As I see it, what takes us past regret is dealing with the choices we make: going beyond guilt, trying to make amends, and, oh yes, occasionally patting yourself on the back for having done it right.

That dreaded trip back to face all the *pésames* (condolences), all the expressions of pity given the way my dad died. Why she took such a long time to return was hard to understand then, but today I have an inkling. My mom survived so much trauma by not dealing with it directly, pretending it never happened, or if it did, suicide was out of the picture. Going back to Spain shortly after my dad's death wouldn't allow her to do that. It was 1974, an intensely trying time in Spanish history, and the intensity was merciful in that it seemed to deflect from the gravitas of our situation. Franco was dying, and another Spain was in the making. Family conversations would rapidly turn from the well-being of my mom to the monumental issue of "Spain after the death of the dictator." The circumstances gave cause for unease, but they were also exciting. My mom thought so too, but by this time in her life, the politics of Spain were not on her mind. Her birthplace had become remote, inconsequential. Ironically, Franco's death was a subject of conversation in which Mercedes did not participate, other than to recall a few incidents of the war years.

Mercedes was looking good when she returned to Spain, the same high-strung Mercedes they were all used to, but nothing out of the ordinary. What I remember most about that trip is the plan the family in Spain had conjured up for my mother. I liked the plan. She would move back, take up residence in our beach place in Alicante, or if not that place—it becomes depressingly isolated in the winter months—perhaps in Alicante city. We even went apartment hunting, and every time the issue arose about Mercedes moving back, all the family members without exception thought it was a great idea. They were impressed by something my mom had agreed to do in one of those trips back after the tragedy: she took care of her stepmother, Mamá Amelia, if only for a few months. I too was impressed, thus the thought of a permanent move back for my mom was attractive, more frequent trips to Spain with my U.S. family, and as a result (I confess), she'd be a lesser burden on my shoulders. Besides, the possibility of my mom taking over the duties of caring for Mamá Amelia was an added benefit. But of course, like so many of our plans for Mercedes, this one fell through. To this day I'm convinced she had no intention of moving back; she just let on that she was thinking of doing so in order to attract attention—she loved conversations in which she was the main thread. My aunt Bea, Artemio Jr.'s wife, had a plan for her. She would move to Spain, and Jorge and Miguel would eventually follow suit.

So there you have it: she would remain in Hanover thinking constantly about her two "boys" and their eventual move to be with her, as she let her mind wander—no job, no hobby, nothing to keep her occupied, utterly alone, with the exception of infrequent visits by those two boys and their families. There's a dimension of my mother's life that's difficult to reveal, but if I left it out, the picture of Mercedes would be utterly incomplete. The relationships between Mercedes and the many (too many?) women to whom her sons had committed themselves at various stages of their lives were atrocious—the source of major family conflicts. Indeed, none of the women we married, divorced, or took up with were on good terms with Mercedes. And the cause of the dysfunction was not two-sided, since they all tried unsuccessfully (at least at first) to make it work. She would needle them, look for their vulnerabilities, and when she found the weaknesses she'd go for the jugular. She often reminded my exes that Maicol had many sweethearts, that he used to go with a "dotter of a dotor," that he had his eye out for someone else, constantly insinuating that I was two-timing. Her comments about her sons' significant others—their clothes, their figures, their hair, their family background and status—were at times coy, sometimes direct, too often meant as a slap in the face. But these conversations took place strategically when I wasn't around, and when I got wind of what my mom was telling these women, I would react badly, which is just what she was looking for— the more drama the better. Maurita (the mother of my son, Francisco, and daughter, Maura), remembers well that when her brother came to Hanover for a visit on a cold New Hampshire night, Mercedes went into his bedroom when he was sleeping, stealthily removed the blanket from his bed, and took it to my bedroom, where she covered me as if I had not yet reached the age of three—after all, Michael was the delicate one, higher class, more sensitive to natural adversities, unlike the family of her daughter-in-law.

What were we going to do about Mercedes? How would we deliver her from her one hundred years of solitude when it was abundantly clear that living with her sons and in-laws was going to be impossible? Mercedes wanted her two boys to herself; sharing was not an option. This situation led to another failed plan for her, this time conjured up by my dad's good friend and colleague at Dartmouth, Bob Russell: she would rent a room in that spacious house on Dana Road to a native-Spanish-speaking student, a high-class Mexican named Sebastián (not his real name).

Meet Sebastián. There he is posing for one of my mom's excruciatingly crude photos taken with a cheap Kodak (an Ektralite 10) for people who have no idea how to take pictures. Tall, a Roman nose—God forbid that he have indigenous features—light skin, a casual brown suit, white shirt, no tie, a stylish haircut that surely cost him a pretty peso, hands on hips, looking haughty. And to top it all off, he was in the Dartmouth engineering school: a hell of an (Ivy League) engineer. My mom took one look at him and thought he would be just fine. Yes, wonderful, just what she needed—a substitute son. But it started to go beyond that; not only was Sebastián her stand-in son, there was always the potential of a "fleert" that would lead to a relationship, which was highly unlikely. I remember I thought at first it was a grand idea, anything to lessen the load that had become my mother, the poor woman whose husband had killed himself, and the woman who, in my mind, was not doing enough to make her own life less lonely. So Sebastián was something of a salvation—until he wasn't.

In addition to all Sebastián's wonderful features, he was charming and worldly, despite his youth. According to Mercedes, *"No parece mexicano"* (Doesn't look Mexican), whatever that means. I'm embarrassed when I think of all the social, political, and racial implications of that phrase. In any case, she was intensely attracted to him, and besides, my dad's colleague and friend of many years had recommended him. But within a few months, he stopped paying the minimal amount that was agreed upon, and his appearance at the house became sporadic. I took a look at my mom's bank account, discovering that not only was he not paying rent, it was my mom who seemed to be paying him. After finding out about that, Sebastián's charm faded. More than that, Sebastián had become a family issue. We—my brother, my wife, and his wife all agreed that he must go. But where? Who could prevent his reentry into our home when we weren't there, and who could keep my mom from writing him checks?

Of course Sebastián would remain in her life as long as he needed support. Apparently, his father had cut him off from the family treasure because he was not studying. My mother told me of Sebastián's difficulties with his father—alienation, misunderstandings. Despite his brilliance, he was not making academic progress. He needed someone who understood him. All this made me even more upset, especially when I saw that he had taken my mother's car for several weeks on a trip to God knows where; I think she said Canada, but who knows? Of course he returned. "That bastard," I would say to myself and to her—a prodigal son who came back not because he saw the error of his ways, but because he needed a free place to crash.

Sebastián aside, another Ugarte family discussion involved the need to move Mercedes to a different home. The house on Dana Road, with two stories and a basement, posed some safety issues for a woman in her late sixties. It was also too big for her and contained lots of not-always-good memories. My brother and I moved her to a house he had found for her on the outskirts of Hanover, in the municipality of West Lebanon, a town whose property taxes were lower than Hanover's. The move was highly upsetting to her, but we did it. Mom was adamantly opposed to moving anywhere, but I sensed she was happy about the attention she got from her two boys: George and Michael working together for the benefit of the family, a fond memory.

A more up-to-date dwelling—all on one floor, not as much maintenance, practical and utterly insipid—would be just what she needed, or so we thought. Never mind that she would no longer be able to walk to town or go to The Hop or to movies. Of course we thought of all that, but the benefits outweighed the drawbacks. One unforeseen benefit was that as a result of the move, she became dear friends with an Italian woman who, with her husband, rented our family home and eventually bought it. Her name was Arianna: kind, gentle, and deeply sympathetic and cognizant of my mother's solitude, for she too had a mother in a similar circumstance in Italy. Another fond memory of those days, along with the fraught ones, were the occasional visits of my nephew, George's son Andrew, who took road trips from Boston College where he was an undergrad to Hanover to visit Grandma, whom he found strange, yet generous and charming. Still, my mom's aloneness living just outside the municipal limit of Hanover would become an even greater burden. Lo and behold, weeks after the move, when I visited her in her new abode, I again saw evidence of Sebastián, and lots of it: boxes, clothes, books, the belongings of a typical student living in a temporary home away from home, with a solicitous substitute mom as an added attraction.

So my brother and I decided to take things into our own hands. We arranged to get together at my mom's new house, gather up all of Sebastian's belongings, rent a truck, and haul off the possessions and deposit them in West Lebanon's municipal dump. I recall this episode as particularly traumatic for my mother. Weeping as we loaded his boxes into the van, she bellowed out how important his projects were, that he was a good boy and that she loved him, a scene right out of the novel by Antonio Gala she was reading at the time. I thought my mom was acting out his novels. *Nos queremos* (We love each other), she blurted out. She was also reenacting the scene circa 1935 when she told her father that she was in love with her uncle. How grotesque all this was to my brother and me.

Taking Sebastián's things to the dump was as cathartic for us as it was an insurmountable injustice for my mom. But nothing changed, as if that was going to solve anything. The cuteness of it all stopped, however, when she revealed to me that Sebastián had slapped her. I felt I had to go a step further, something I'm not at all proud of. I wrote him a letter, hand-delivered by Mercedes, in which I told him that if he continued to take advantage of my dear mother, I would alert the immigration authorities, since she had told me that his immigration status was precarious because he was no longer taking courses. I felt I had to do anything to protect my mother, no matter if it went against my political and social principles. That letter seemed to work; Mercedes told me that when she gave it to him, he grimaced, and left. For good? Who knows if he returned? In any case, my mom spoke less of him after this scene. But her pain at the breakup would not last; years later, she took up with another handsome young man, equally enchanting and equally interested in Mercedes' purchasing power.

His name could have been Paulino or Pablo. (I know his real name, but I'd rather not divulge it.) His behavior was either borderline criminal or 100 percent delinquent. She met him in 1985. I was in Madrid on a sabbatical year of my own, doing research on Spanish Civil War exile literature, an issue that had direct bearing on my family. It was for me a great opportunity to live in one of Europe's most vibrant cities with my family. Both my children barely spoke a word of Spanish before that year, and after, they had become nearly fluent. When Grandma spoke Spanish to them, now they could reply in Spanish. What a wonderful chance for Mercedes (now seventy-two) to make new contact with her family.

But wait a minute: it would have been more wonderful were it not for the glaring fact that Mercedes had so alienated the mother of my children that living under the same roof would be an absolute impossibility. So the negotiation was that my mom would come to Madrid and stay a few months at a hotel suite I had set up for her near where we were living in the neighborhood of Chamberí. Mercedes was my responsibility; it was up to me to make sure she was taken care of and spending "quality time" (what a euphemism!) with us. Sure enough, Mercedes, not within my supervision at all times, made friends with a young man of thirty or so in an apartment-hotel close to the Plaza of Alonso Martínez. Paulino—another good-looking "simpatico" chatty guy interested in my mom in a way resembling Sebastián's need for cash. She told me about him, that he worked or knew someone who worked at the *aparto-hotel*, and I was curious, happy she had made a friend, yet deeply suspicious, considering her previous fling with Sebastián. I don't remember how long it took for her to get robbed. Memory tells me it happened in one of Madrid's major landmarks—the Puerta del Sol, the Retiro Park, or Plaza Mayor. Her purse was snatched. Notice I use the passive voice, not doubt my intent to be impartial, more like an admission that I have no proof. But chances are very likely—as virtually all my family members in Spain assumed—that Paulino had set up the snatch, and the perpetrator was in cahoots with him.

"Don't let that guy anywhere near your mother," advised my aunt Marina when she got wind of it. My mother told her about it in what her sister related to me as a rambling monologue about a cute guy she had met in Madrid who expressed indignation to her that someone had grabbed her purse. I also was indignant, as was my ex, whereas others in my family smiled ironically when I told them about it—a typical Madrid happening—goes on all the time. Maybe the only compensation is that the accompanying physical violence is rare, and Mercedes was fortunate that nothing like that happened. Mercedes forgot about it almost immediately; she was only carrying some four thousand pesetas (before the euro) worth about thirty dollars, and she did not use credit cards. Anything having to do with money, no matter the currency, was beyond her. She would "go out" with Paulino several times after that despite, or maybe because of, what we told her about him. Was she thinking of her father's resistance to her own relationship with Paco?

Paulino would remain on her mind for many years, well into her eighties, even nineties. He inspired her writing as well as her reading. I don't know for sure, but I strongly suspect that her interest in the romance novelist, Antonio Gala, came from Paulino. I also surmise that Paulino was gay: she told me he had a deep interest in Pedro Almodóvar (a gay flame at that time), and when I spoke to the personnel at the *aparto-hotel* about unimportant matters like payment or the whereabouts of my mom when she was not in her room, they would say she left with Paulino, and the way they said it—a certain knowing gaze—made me wonder about him. In the long run, I have no idea who Paulino really was; what I do know is that Mercedes had conjured up a bad romance novel about her relationship with him, the main conduit of which was her many communications with him through letters and phone calls. Yes, many of them. I saw her phone bills and her notebooks; all of these, with no exception, revealed strictly one-way communications. If Paulino ever returned a call, or if they actually spoke on the phone, I will never know for sure, but I don't think so. And the notebooks—containing rough drafts of letters to her "Querido Paulino" in which she relates virtually nothing—show her interest but not a great deal of detail.

There are pages and pages of "Querido Paulino . . . today Miguel and I went for coffee, I had a croissant and he a slice of toast. We then went shopping for light bulbs . . ." and so on. That one was from Missouri, but she had many of them from her house in West Lebanon, New Hampshire, too. After she died I spent many hours sifting through those notebooks looking for an epistolary romance novel, with verbal sighs, memories of holding hands, a smile, a tear in the knowledge that one of them must leave, a realization that it was an impossible affair, something out of *The Bridges of Madison County*. But nothing like that. If I can relate something in film that reminded me of Mercedes' worse-than-eccentric behavior, it would be when the wife of the pathological killer in *The Shining*, totally bonkers, discovers that the novel he says he has been writing for the last months consists of pages and pages of the same sentence written over and over. That's not exactly Mercedes, but it's clear that those one hundred years of solitude did something to her. How to occupy her time alone all day? she asked. I would suggest, "Why not write your ideas, your emotions, your life?" And she did.

But she didn't. I haven't stopped looking for the pages that demonstrate her ingeniousness, her sense of wordplay and absurdity, the verbal quirkiness she was known for. Every now and then, however, I found written evidence of just that; it's in her little notes, her one-liners written on napkins and *Time* magazine inserts, or in books, like when she scribbled on the dedication page of the book I was writing while we were in Madrid when she met Paulino. I dedicated it to my father and all of his ilk, the emigrant-exiles: "In memory of my father, Francisco Ugarte, one more in the long line of Spanish émigrés from fascist Spain." Mercedes wrote on that page: "And where is he now, Tarzan in Manhattan?" This is in English. Yes, Tarzan in Manhattan, a reminder of Paco in New York after that last trip to Spain? Tarzan: the strongman protector of jungle flora and fauna and pretty princesses in danger of being swallowed up by dangerous creatures. Instead of protecting her, now he was looking after damsels in Manhattan. Yes, interpreting my mom's words was at times like interpreting a deliberately whimsical surrealist poem.

Maybe the greatest (and grandest) happening during her hundred lonely years was the Thanksgiving celebration of that year in Spain with my family: 1985. Maurita and I wanted to return the generosity of my uncle Artemio and his family, who had invited us to many dinners and good times in their retreat outside Madrid. We would do so with a U.S. style Thanksgiving dinner. I had rented a car presuming that Spanish auto rental agencies made sure to fill the gas tanks of their vehicles before letting them into the streets and byways of Spain. Wrong presumption, nothing doing. We ran out of gas on a road only a few kilometers from a town on the way to my uncle's place. So it was up to my son and me to trek off to the town while Maurita, who was not fond of Mercedes, waited with our daughter in the car parked on the shoulder of the country road. It took Francisco and me over an hour to find a kind soul to help us. In the meantime, back on the road, my libido-filled mother decided to seek help by approaching the edge of the road (mercifully not a highway). As cars passed, she raised her skirt to the thigh, exposing her seventy-two-year-old leg—something out of *It Happened One Night*—a proverbial sight for sore (and stunned) eyes among those motorists who probably thought

Spain had been invaded by Martians. What was she thinking?

When Francisco and I got back to the car with a generous person from the next town who luckily had a spare gallon of gas, I noticed my mom's sly smile and Maura, who was only seven, looking perplexed. We made it to my uncle's place but not exactly on time. Maurita's knowing glance at me made me think something strange had happened. "Ay, Mercedes," I recall my cousin Amaya saying when Maurita and I told the eagerly waiting family what had happened. There was hearty laughter in the midst of those mischievous twinkling eyes of Mercedes as she again made it abundantly clear that her love-spirit had not subsided one single degree since the death of her Paco.

Could this incident have been related in an Antonio Gala novel my mom was reading? Perhaps not, since the incidents in those novels tend to be plausible; this, I affirm, was not plausible—although true. Mercedes was eager to be the protagonist of a romance novel. Going forward in this epic love tale, several years after her sons' cruel prohibition of her relationship with the young Mexican stud, along with the episode of the raised skirt, she met the romance novelist Gala. It was at the Madrid Book Fair, a grandiose annual event at the Retiro Park in Madrid lasting almost a month: over a thousand booths selling all genres of books, new and used; authors making appearances, signing autographs, speaking to their readers; publishers trying to make deals; would-be authors trying to sell their writing. It's a happening that countless Spaniards from all over the country attend, valiantly struggling against the global tendency to do away with the printed word. There are book fairs all over Spain, but this one, due to Madrid's centrality and publishing dominance, is perhaps the most prominent. So in the mid-nineties Mercedes and I joined the book fair crowds on one of our trips back to Spain during the spring and summer months. By this time my mom was in her eighties, slowing down significantly. With her dysfunctional hearing aid often at the point of falling out, unkempt hair, a blouse and jacket she had bought at Wal-Mart a decade ago, arm in arm with her son, she was no longer a woman of Spain, or so I thought. Sadly, it's possible she would have been better off if she and Paco had stayed in Spain. Certainly there would have been many antidotes to her loneliness: shops close to living spaces, more contact with people, other widows sipping coffee at a sidewalk terraza, complaining about how little they see their grandchildren. Only once a week. This could all have been true, but it didn't happen.

Here we were, eying the booths, stopping for moments to look at covers, gawking at the few celebrities who happened to be around signing autographs. Suddenly, over the loudspeaker, we heard it—or I heard it, because my mom was oblivious to loudspeakers and virtually all public announcements—Antonio Gala was signing books at booth number five hundred and whatever. "*Oye, Mamá, a que no sabes quién está firmando hoy*" (Hey, Mom, guess who's signing today). "*Pues vamos*" (Let's go). I think we said this in unison. But when we arrived at booth five hundred and whatever, my heart sunk when I saw the long line of autograph-seekers, *all* of whom were women from ages 55 to 103.

Mercedes would be thrilled to say a few words to the author of *La regla de tres* (*The Rule of Three*). In line we waited and waited, and when it was our turn, Mercedes bellied up to the table where Antonio and his agents seemed to be having a gay old time expressing thanks to the admirers. A handsome man he was, dark, Andalusian, aging gracefully with a seemingly eternal smile. But I'm not sure he expected anyone like Mercedes. In contrast to the demure, blushing ladies, nearly speechless in his presence, Mercedes went up to him, pounded her fist on his table, something that startled all of those who witnessed it, including me, and said, "*Oye, tú no sabes nada de lo que fue la guerra, yo la viví y sé lo que pasó*" (Hey, you don't know a thing about the war, I lived it, and I know what happened). Antonio Gala was born in 1930, so my mom was not technically correct—he was a lad of six when the war began, so he must have known something about it. To this day, I'm not sure what provoked those words and that defiance, only that it was in some ways typical of Mercedes in her persistent thirst for attention; she wanted to let Antonio and those around her know she was within earshot as she often repeated a phrase right out of one of Antonio Gala's titles, *Ahora hablaré de mí* (And Now I'll Talk about Myself). And it was indeed time for Mercedes to talk about herself, her real self, her desires, her frustrations, her likes and hopes. It's time for others to shut up, including Gala.

Well, Antonio could not have been more gracious. At first taken aback by this seemingly crazy woman yet unwilling to step away, as one of his aids had coaxed him to do, he answered her, saying that indeed, the war remained a childhood memory to him and that more people like you, señora, should write about it. With her typically mischievous-victorious expression, Mercedes slipped him a piece of paper—maybe a napkin, since we had not brought a copy of one of his books—while I retreated, utterly embarrassed by her behavior. On that makeshift writing surface he wrote a note to Mercedes, encouraging her to write about her experiences. "With much gratitude." But for what? The gratitude I think came from Mercedes' son, thankful that Gala had not dismissed her.

I wonder if the Gala experience had anything to do with the aloneness. The years of Mercedes living in the house in West Lebanon were marked by her growing confusion about the space she was inhabiting, as well as by visits, much too infrequent, from her family and the few friends still alive. My son Francisco was a student at a college in Maine, and his then-girlfriend had friends in the "Upper Valley" of the Connecticut River separating New Hampshire and Vermont. For me, the situation was perfect; they visited her every now and then, despite her increasing weirdness, and best of all, they all seemed to love these vacations. Grandma had turned into the eccentric lady whose behavior was unpredictable and often ludicrously inexplicable. Her interior decorating, if that's what you could call it, was like something out of an absurdist play: chairs on top of a sofa, paper napkins strategically placed on walls as if they were portraits, issues of *Time* magazine everywhere. She refused to throw away anything. I believe my son was more tolerant of her than I.

Oil portrait of Mercedes by Sedsil Nelson circa 1957

Starting in the nineties and well into the next century, my sense of my mom was that she was not aging gracefully. She looked nothing like the image of Mercedes in the painting of her that had hung in our family home. That 1957 portrait, a soothing picture of her in a black lace dress that made her look like a prominent Spanish lady—sky blue background, a brunette smiling, lips red, hands folded in front of her, a wedding band tastefully and subtly shining on her finger at the bottom of the painting—that picture was not the Mercedes of the photos my daughter took of her in the years after her last move, the one to Missouri in 1998. That lady stood out too in 1998, but it was a different Mercedes.

Chapter Eleven

Golden (Not-So-Golden) Years in Missouri

The move from New Hampshire to Missouri was in the summer of 1998. It was exciting, exhausting, emotionally draining, sometimes enjoyable, and mostly hellish. But who am I talking about? My mother or myself? Yes, the move was hellish for me as well as for my brother and his son Chris, because everything seemed to turn into an argument with Mercedes—sometimes yelling, sometimes tears, sometimes laughing, sometimes dramatic sighs with eyes rolling nearly out of her sockets. George and Chris had come to West Lebanon to load the moving van and then to Missouri to unload it. I was in charge of transporting Mercedes from New Hampshire to Missouri. But am I sure the move away from all she was familiar with was infernal for her? After all, she was in her element: her two boys and grandson fussing over her, making plans with an eye toward a better life for everybody, giving advice she would never take. Life could not have been better, regardless of all the exasperation. The truth is that we all rose to the occasion of looking after the Ugarte Precioso matriarch. I think that move drew me closer to my brother and his youngest son.

There were many trying incidents. *"Mamá, esto no vale nada"* (Mom, this is worth nothing). It was a cardboard box of souvenirs, postcards, old pens that didn't write, picture frames with no pictures, napkins, old scarves, and other things whose combined proper name was junk. *"Mamá eso es basura; lo voy a llevar al basurero"* (Mom, that's trash, I'm taking it to the trash can or the dump). As I made my way to the trash, she screamed, *"No lo tires. Es mío. Son mis cosas de toda la vida"* (Don't throw it away. It's mine. My things of all my life). She would say this several times in varying forms, tears in her eyes. My response was *"Lágrimas de cocodrilo"* (Crocodile tears), and I did not hesitate as I trudged straight to the trash. After that I decided to throw things away without telling her. Her wardrobe, moth-eaten, costume-like, blouses of a different epoch, dresses out of the films of Frank Capra. Old pots she never used because she had stopped cooking years earlier. If it weren't for Meals on Wheels, she might not have made it to age eighty. And all those issues of *Time* magazine. I can't say which was the earliest one I found, but I can say that some of those magazines ran back as far as the days when my dad was alive. He was an avid reader of *Time*; she read them too, but she stuck to the "People" section and an occasional movie review she couldn't quite make sense of. But she loved the covers: dramatic photos of prominent people, most of whom she recognized. And for the ones she didn't, she would have a comment on their appearance: too fat, nice face with no body, no chest, chest too big, blond, dark, ugly, or glamorous. After the move, canceling her subscription was not to her liking. When Kate Winslet made the front cover for her role in *Titanic*, she was thrilled. It was her favorite movie for many years; Leonardo DiCaprio, her favorite hunk in those days, reminded her of the many young men she called her "fleerts."

As Mercedes' life became more precarious, as she treaded onward with lessening physical balance, her hearing, along with her other senses, diminishing, she became more dependent on me, and as I attended to her with a new intensity, I ultimately became more dependent on her. It was a case of codependence to use the pop scientific lingo of today. She needed me for obvious reasons, but not so obvious was why I needed her. Possible reasons: to resolve a conflict with her that began the moment I was born, to show the world I was a good person, to learn of my family history from an eyewitness, to speak in a quotidian way in the language of my ancestors, *"Mamá, me voy a correr; o me voy corriendo"* (Mom, I'm going for a run; I mean I'm taking off). And her answer was, *"A ver lo que haces"* (untranslatable, literally, it means "Let's see what you do," but it was more like, "Be careful, cause I don't trust you"). But of all those reasons, the strongest was my need to resolve that life tension with her—the reason also for writing this book.

Several weeks before the move I arranged her things into three piles of junk: Pile A for the trash pick-up, Pile B for Goodwill, and Pile C for the essentials that would end up in the moving van and ultimately her new residence. Making the determination of which pile was appropriate for each one of her million possessions was tortuous and time-consuming, but I was the decider. Those decisions had to be tyrannical. At first, I thought she must at least have a say in what she wanted to keep, but when she tearfully insisted on taking every single issue of *Time* magazine with her to Missouri, I decided it was time for a seizure of power. The photos were my only weakness. I think I put every one of them in Pile C—essential, unless you believe that your memories are disposable.

The three-day, two-night trip to Missouri in a 1988 Chevette with no air conditioning in August was as infernal for me as it was fun for her. She enjoyed the road trip over the highways of Vermont, New York, Pennsylvania, Ohio, Indiana, Illinois, and finally Missouri. The temperature ranged from high eighties to ninety-five Fahrenheit, and I don't do well in the heat, but she seemed fine. She soon forgot all those precious objects she would never see again, as she let go of her past. And the reality of being with her Miguel was something that she had wanted for a long time—her two boys were her *raison d'être*. My conclusion today is that she had a grand time on that trip. One of our stops for lunch was in a roadside park in Who-Knows-Where, upstate New York. It was off the highway—woods, rolling hills, and a little pond close by. I had packed a baguette, wine, and cheese. I remember asking her: *"¿Te acuerdas, cuando Jorge y yo éramos pequeños—esos viajes por las carreteras de Francia con Papá?"* (Do you remember those road trips with Dad through France when George and I were little?).

I had gotten to a point with my mom where I needed her to remember her past, as much for me as for her. Many of us reach that point with our moms and dads, and I sense they all respond in different ways. Mercedes just smiled and went along with my memory, not hers. She was surrendering to me; proof was the way her memory coalesced with mine. The French baguette, *foie gras*, Roquefort cheese, and at a younger-than-drinking age, they allowed my brother and me to sip the wine; and those French towns you could see many miles away from the rural roads—this was before divided highways—because the church or cathedral of each town stood out over the horizon. I can taste the Roquefort and the bread from the *boulangerie* of the previous village as I gaze at photos of the majesty of those churches. Nostalgia is at its best when you remember things together with someone who was there. "*¿Te acuerdas, Mamá?*" (Do you remember, Mom?) Nostalgia might be, as Zora Neale Hurston says, the property of women. But it's also a shared experience, and on this trip from New Hampshire to Missouri, I laid claim to that property.

For the next eight years she lived about a mile from my house; those years were mostly wonderful. Her two-bedroom apartment was in a complex of units each with a small patio, wall-to-wall carpet, a functional kitchen-dining room, and in the backyard, an artificial pond inhabited by migrating geese, some of whom decided to forsake the rest of their trip and stay in this comfortable niche. For a woman in her eighties she was in remarkably good health; the only medication she took was for hypothyroid. Everything else, except for an occasional delusion, was just fine. She was lucky to have a wonderful gerontologist, Dr. David Mehr, who spoke Spanish to her. She was thrilled to answer his questions about her sleeping, diet, and daily activities (or lack thereof); her dark Spanish eyes, still sparkling despite her age, lit up. She made up the answers to these questions when she insisted she was eating very, very well, "*muy muy bien porque Miguel me da de comer*" (because Michael feeds me). This was true, but it was a major chore, because she insisted on stuffing her mouth with all those milk chocolate bars. "Heershees" she called them. "*Mamá, no más*" (Mom, no more) I told her with no consequence.

But my frustration level was tested every day. I always asked her what she would like to eat, and she nearly always answered, "*nada.*" So I cooked something for both of us. I put a plate of pasta, or beans and rice, or a slice of *tortilla de patatas* in front of her, and her response was nearly always that she didn't want anything, but within a few minutes, she gobbled it down. She seldom left anything on her plate. I managed to figure out the several degrees of "no" that my mom used when I asked her if she wanted anything. A "no" with little or no inflection meant yes, a "no" with a touch of severity meant probably, a genuinely severe "no" meant maybe, and a loud "NO" with a dramatic flair suggesting impending death meant no. I remember tossing some parsley leaves into her salad one day, and her reaction was, "NO, parsley causes paralysis." She said this in English, with her Spanish inflections. I don't know where she got this, but I suspect it had to do with her remarkable predilection for alliteration and linguistic cadences. Of course, parsley and paralysis; it works in Spanish too. How could it be otherwise? She once made my daughter Maura (or Molly as we called her then) keel over in laughter when she confused the number eight, the verb ate, and the colloquial contraction ain't, all together. "Molly, we ain't chicken." "You mean we ate chicken or had eight chickens?" What we all remember is the laughter—both my children had a fun time (albeit exasperating) conversing with Grandma Mercedes. So did I, more so as she got older. I was approaching that place in which I was comfortable with her. I suspect that had to do with the fact that we both let go. She allowed me to help her, and I allowed her to be the wild and crazy woman she had always been.

It was at this time, around 2005, when Maura took some penetrating photos of her in all my daughter's tender professionalism. My mom had been living in Missouri for several years. Maura was tracking her in her deterioration. It was a series of black and white photos that reflected her life better than any picture of her Grandma I have seen. Mercedes' memory and her mental state were becoming more and more precarious. One never knows how people with dementia really feel because, like children, articulating emotions is something exasperatingly difficult. Children get better at it with age, while those suffering from senile dementia get worse as the years pile on. Maura's photos, along with those in our family album, speak with great eloquence.

Here is Mercedes in her room sitting in a propped-up bed-chair, wearing an elaborately knitted white sweater with shiny buttons, the cuffs doubled back. The background—a couple of pictures on the wall, a lamp I barely recognize from many years ago—is not in focus. The focus is on Mercedes in her eighties in a pose we in the family are all familiar with. In all her movie-star drama and coquettishness, she smiles. It's the same smile she offers the camera as the one where she holds her pure white-haired second-born son up like a trophy. Her left arm is behind her head in that gesture of "look at me in all my glamour," Bette Davis style, or Lana Turner, or Elizabeth Taylor. It was a pose she performed to the hilt. Her hair is unkempt, in stark contrast to the images of half a century earlier, as if she were highlighting (unwittingly) the contrast between then and now.

Turning the page of the photo album, there are other eight-by-ten-inch images of Mercedes looking very confused. She seems not to know where she is. In one she is looking down, her mouth slightly open in what looks like a frown. Her right hand is raised as far as her chest; the wrinkles of that hand are the center of the photo. Again her hair is so disheveled that she looks something like a bag lady wearing a housecoat from her ancient wardrobe. Above is another photo, a portrait of her when she was about forty-six: utterly beautiful, a Spanish lady from La Mancha, dark, smiling, wearing an elegant black dress open at the neck. In that picture within the picture, her hairdo, a perfect continuation of the dress, is no doubt the creation of an expert stylist. What I love about this portrait is that my mother does not seem to flaunt her appearance. She is a good mom, and at the same time she is an elegant Spanish lady. That's what I wanted my mom to be, and that's what I wanted others to see. But forty years later, here she is in another photo suffering from dementia.

There are also several glimpses of my mom's possessions, in all their ordinariness—an unmade single bed, the one she had lain in for decades, alongside the other single bed in which her husband had slept. Yes, I recognize them—we brought those beds all the way from New Hampshire—also blankets, clothes, papers, a phone that didn't work, bathroom items like unused toothbrushes still in the package, an artificial flower, a two-by-five religious card of an unnamed virgin, halo and all, scotch-taped onto the mirror, and right next to it a bottle of Tums.

Yes, here they are, a few of those things I wanted her to throw away when she moved from New Hampshire to Missouri; she kept them without my knowing it, imitating (unwittingly?) me when I threw things out without her knowing it. There she is in another one, a candid shot watching television. There is a glaring image on the TV that dominates the photo: a twenty-something pretty blond trying to look glamorous. The young lady seems to avoid the gaze of my frowning mother. My mom doesn't seem to be enjoying herself; she loved glamour, but it seems that this young woman is conveying to her that she is not glamorous. On the walls are the pictures of the past, it's a photo of photos. There is my uncle as a young man about to go to war, another one of Mercedes with her sister Marina and brother Artemio—all three in their seventies—and what looks like a very old picture of two young girls, one of whom must have been my mom when she was around ten.

The photo that most affects me was taken by my daughter, Maura. It says everything about my relationship with my mom in those years. She is at the dinner table in my dining room during one of those many weekends when she came over to my house. I am bending over her as I wrap a bib around her neck and upper body. She looks slightly uncomfortable because I'm sure the thought of eating did not make her happy. Behind her is my bookshelf. She liked the shelves of books because no doubt they reminded her of her years in Hanover with Paco. But then again, that's my supposition; maybe it's wishful remembering. Wine glasses, cloth napkins, silverware, and a dish of what looks like rice. I loved cooking *paella* for her, even though she complained. Invariably she ate it in spite of herself. In the photo I see that both my mom and I look tired. Tired of old age? Both of us getting old. Tired of repeating our patterns. Tired of talking to each other.

When I first saw the photo, I hated it. It features my bald head and an awkward gesture as I attend to the bib that will protect my mom's clothes from spills, drools, or unchewed food. I am wearing clothes much too big for me, and my mom is in her old-lady rags. But in the long run, the photo shows me who I was at that time, a man intensely interested in his mother's welfare, perhaps as way to make up for her hundred years of solitude. A photographer must be sensitive to the moment, an observer, a technician of the camera, in some cases an artist whose craft is to depict emotion at a dramatic instant. Neither Mercedes nor Miguel knew that Maura was looking at us in that way, and even less that she was doing so behind a camera lens. But my daughter got it right, so much so that I balked at my first glimpse and then understood the affection when I really looked at the picture. The lesson? Forgive the preachiness, but our moms deserve a closer look than we might give them. My daughter knew how to look at Mercedes.

In those years I remember jogging close to her apartment and seeing a family of deer—not the least bit uncommon for those environs. Civilization and lack of predators had led them to seek sustenance in garbage areas of apartment complexes like this one—close to nature, but not too close. My mother fit in well, both with the geese and the deer, or so I thought as I described her new abode to those who cared about her in Spain thousands of miles (and years) away. In my mind, things could not have been better for Mercedes at this time. But again, all this is much more my memory than hers.

My daughter was living in Chicago at the time studying documentary film with occasional visits to Columbia, so Mercedes and I took several trips to Chicago via Amtrak to see her, eight hours in a rickety train stopping in no-name towns and cities in Missouri and Illinois. There we were on a train en route to Chicago on a December day in the middle of a cornfield whose corn had gone to seed. Northern Missouri is relatively flat, like La Mancha, but the corn and soybean fields of Missouri are no competition for those of Illinois, and in the winter on a train, looking out into that bleak flatness seemed so utterly distant from my mom's place of birth.

It started to snow, at first lightly, then it came down heavily, and the memories were ignited: New Hampshire, the first snow of the year, Mercedes on skis, Mercedes sending pictures of herself on skis to her family in Hellín, Michael and George throwing snowballs, Cisco skating on Occom pond with Stephanie, and Omar Sharif. Yes, the vast expanses of Illinois corn fields reminded her of *Dr. Zhivago* and Omar Sharif on a horse galloping from his snow-covered family estate where he lived with his wife and children to a nearby town to be with his mistress. She loved *Dr. Zhivago*, the movie, particularly the Zhivago played by the Egyptian hunk; she loved him in another epic, *Lawrence of Arabia*. But now she was in the middle of a snowy field on a northbound train, going to what was to her an exotic place: Chicago.

I too was pleasantly surprised by the newly fallen snow; in less than an hour that cornfield had turned into the Russian steppes, soothing in its suggestion of infinity along with all those memories of her adopted home in New Hampshire in the 1950s and 60s. I recall I was on the verge of sleep, but not Mercedes. I was rudely yanked from much-needed shut-eye by an old lady bellowing out the theme of *Dr. Zhivago* as she gazed out the window smiling that naughty smile of hers, not the least bit embarrassed that she did not have a pleasant voice and was singing so far out of key that I saw a little girl on the train bring her hands to her ears. Not only was she oblivious to her immediate surroundings on the train, but the everyday protocols of normal behavior were of little consequence. Yet I preferred, both then and now, to see my mom's behavior as the mark of an acute sensitivity to her outside surroundings, to her memories, to the wonderment of the first snow viewed from this privileged position in the middle of Nowhere, Illinois.

I was becoming less embarrassed by Mercedes' behavior. I tried to see what she saw, and I was learning from the attempt. That trip to Chicago, my mom belting out the theme from *Dr. Zhivago*, could have been the definitive moment when I decided I would write about her. It took me many years, really my entire life, to see the world with her eyes. Not that I saw clearly— God knows what she saw with those eyes of a girl of five who lost her mom to a strange illness, a recent bride whose dad was sentenced to death, or a woman whose husband threw himself into a gorge. But the point is that I was trying to see it, and it took that tune from *Dr. Zhivago* to allow me to understand that at least I was trying. But don't get your hopes up: I did not sing along with her, not on your life. I just smiled and gently told her to keep it down.

The decade of her life in Columbia, Missouri, provided something of a palliative to the aloneness. I saw her nearly every day, and on weekends we would go to the center of town for coffee or lunch or for a walk on streets that reminded her of the college town of Hanover. Every time we came across someone I knew, which was often after decades of teaching in the university, I introduced her. Invariably she smiled and batted her eyelashes if the one I presented to her was a male under the age of fifty. And if they spoke Spanish, which was often, the better for all involved. She often had something naughty to say, like, "Where is your companion?" or, to someone of the male persuasion, "Do you have a fleert?" or, to a woman, "Maicol ees marri-éd (three syllables), but hees wife ees not heer," as if she were encouraging the beginning of an adulterous romance. The rumors that Professor Ugarte was gay circulated: he was always with his mother, he says he has a "wife" that lives many miles away, and he's not disposed to making eyes at anyone of the opposite sex. Not that I didn't think of it, and not that I didn't "makes eyes" in my own way.

Skip ahead to her funeral, some five years after that train to Chicago and back. I had thought about a service for her well before she died, thinking that few people would attend, perhaps not even her grandchildren—after all, they were so busy. Gloomy thinking: the memorial service of a lonely woman who had led a fascinating event-filled life that no one knew or cared about, especially in this Midwestern college town, so far away from Hellín or from

Hanover. I was sure no one would come. But I was utterly mistaken. Why did I think that her grandchildren on my side would be too busy to come? Both my children dropped everything they were doing to travel to Columbia for the ceremony and both spoke at the service in ways that make me tremble as I write. Many others came to her funeral, much to my amazement, she must have left an impression. It was another marker of my misunderstanding of her (and my) reality. It had paid off for me to have told my students, colleagues, and friends that my mom was living in Columbia. I had invited her to a couple of my classes as an audio-visual aid—a living artifact who had survived the Spanish Civil War. And of course she was delighted to be the center of attention in those class sessions. Francisco's and Maura's mother was there too, despite all the grief and animosity that Mercedes had fomented. Maurita's words made lots of people laugh. As most of us admit, funerals are a time to forget the bad, despite the term "memorial service": forget the burdens and remember (falsely?) the joys.

Yet allow me to jump around in my memories; let's not allow Mercedes to leave this life yet. Back in Columbia, in the first years of the twenty-first century, my mom and I not only enjoyed our coffees in the student cafés, we planned trips to Spain. She was still able to make the journey, and I was somewhat less able to take care of her. On one of those final trips back home to Alicante, I was as exhausted as usual, perhaps this time even more. On our arrival, I helped her up the stairs from the parking lot of the apartment building to the terrace overlooking the Mediterranean. I was way too tired to take in the seaside beauty, even after many months in the Midwest—but not Mercedes. She stopped, dropped the small handbag she was carrying, extended her arms in a pose of the Virgin Mary imitating what they had done to her son, and yelled out to the sea waters, to the palm trees, to the few dolphins that remain in those waters, to the world or to anyone who happened to be listening, "*¡Aún no soy cadáver!*" (I'm not a cadaver yet!). And to those waters, palm trees, and dolphins who were English-speaking, she yelled, "Ees gooood to be alaheeve." My son and daughter repeat it when they remember Grandma. It was becoming a refrain. Today I say it before I fall asleep at night, even the times when I'm not convinced it's true.

My memory of Mercedes begins with a sickness, and I'm afraid that's where it will end. Those "golden years" could not last, especially after she had reached ninety. I remember her ninetieth birthday. 2003. Mercedes had become such an item of curiosity to several of my colleagues—her naughtiness, particularly to the women, her sexual innuendos, her coquettishness, all of which to me were becoming less grotesque. That's not only a statement of fact, it's a confession. The grotesque is in the eye of the beholder, and that beholder had begun to accept his mom as she was. With my help, my colleagues organized a birthday party for her: a couple of Brazilian women and one from Valladolid. Pardon the stereotype, but Brazilians, most of the ones I have met, are the first to acknowledge sexuality as a human trait with no beginning and no end, its joy, its affirmation of life. I do not fault anyone who reads this and concludes that I've fallen into cultural simplemindedness, but then again, Brazil is the land of carnival and the carnivalesque. My mother was a walking carnival; in her youth, the Madrid carnival (or Mardi Gras to those in New Orleans) was known for its transgression of social norms in preparation for the austerity of Lent. Indeed, those transgressions were a vital part of the life and work of her father, Artemio Sr.

But not only Brazilians came to the party. Several of my students came, their spouses, their "fleerts," and maybe even children. Champagne, an artfully baked cake, *tortilla de patatas*, tapas, but most important was the banter, the joy, the recognition of ninety years of life, and the truism that no matter what difficulties we go through—age, want, war, death of loved ones, maladies—there is always something to counter those hardships. And in my mother's case, no one could have said that in the long run she was not a deeply fortunate woman.

But then came more failing health. Her memory had already begun to fail; around age ninety-one it had taken a trip away from my mom's head, and it kept lengthening the distance. The familiar traits of dementia: repeating the same sentence time and time again, asking the same question, not eating properly, constipation, loss of balance, loss of hearing despite a hearing aid (*trompetilla* we called it instead of *audífono*, the former is the word for that awkwardly large horn used in the nineteenth century), we all had to shout to be heard by Mercedes. And worst of all was the lack of attention to her own hygiene.

I needed help. Enter the "helping professions" into Mercedes' life: organizations like Help at Home and Home Instead. That was going to be a problem for many reasons: Mercedes never admitted she needed help, and her never-ending mistrust of people she didn't know—in addition to further loss of the English language—would make it difficult for "outsiders" to do things for her. She was regressing into an earlier life.

Eldercare workers with a knowledge of Spanish in Columbia, Missouri, at that time were a rare commodity. Nonetheless, I thought it would be nice if Mercedes' part-time caretaker could speak Spanish. But at Home Instead there didn't seem to be anyone to fit the description. That was fortunate for us, because the woman who entered my mom's life through Home Instead was Judy—a caring, positive, patient, and helpful woman in the extensive line of people responsible for the long life of Mercedes Precioso. And my mom loved her, no doubt about this one. Mercedes was a woman who could be cantankerous, suspicious, and sometimes mean-spirited with every continuing day until her death. She was a hard pill to swallow, but Judy found her unique, someone she was not accustomed to. And truth be told, there was always something about Mercedes, despite the mean spirit, that made her remarkably charming. These were the penultimate years of my mom's life, from about 2003 to 2005, the year Mercedes took up residence in a nursing home. Even after that move, Judy continued to see her. Judy took her everywhere—coffee shops, grocery stores, parks, the library, the senior center, the hairdresser. Judy was a friend to Mercedes, maybe the best one she ever had in her long life from Hellín to New Hampshire to Missouri. That's a lot of years, and that's a lot of friends; some good ones—caring, intimate—others more indifferent, and still others who were sons of bitches. But among all of them, maybe it was Judy who understood Mercedes the best; indeed more than me, because with me there was too much baggage.

Later, as we realized that my mom needed even more attention, we found another wonderful caregiver. Her name was Frieda, a Mexican woman. I was optimistic, especially in light of the name. Although she spelled her name "Frieda" instead of Frida (as in Kahlo), she was aware of her painterly and vibrant namesake, *muy mexicana* (very Mexican) my mom would say, whatever that means—feisty, intelligent, and so very kind and affectionate. She was several months pregnant, and while my mom was very suspicious of her at first, they became great friends. I told my mom about the acclaimed woman painter and her relationship with the two-timing Diego Rivera, famous for his murals and denunciations of U.S. capitalism. Mercedes was intrigued, but when I showed her a photo of Kahlo as well as her self-portraits, she looked away without saying anything. Kahlo, I surmised, was way too Mexican-looking, which is code for too indigenous. Frieda, on the other hand, was whiter, and when she demonstrated a certain Hispanic warmth when speaking to someone the age of her mom, Mercedes succumbed. I would like to think that Mercedes would have succumbed no matter what Frieda looked like, especially given an inevitable affection that comes with the contact of Spanish-speaking people living in a place that hears the Spanish language as the tongue of the "other."

Frieda's and Mercedes' strolls in the downtown area, coffee, and lots of ice cream made Mercedes look forward to Frieda's visits. But those encounters weren't always good. Frieda was the first to articulate an obvious problem, obvious to everyone, Judy too. My mom was not bathing, and she lied like the proverbial trooper when she told us we needn't worry, that she took a bath every day. Now the dilemma was how to solve that problem short of forcing her into the shower. We never figured that out.

I remember Frieda's notes to me, remarkably well written, wide stroke in her penmanship, probably the product of a convent school. In one of those notes she told me my mom refused to bathe. Somehow Mercedes intercepted that note and wrote a note of her own on the same page: *"Yo estoy bien y los unos y los otros. A mi edad tiene que ser así* (I'm fine, and everyone else is too. At my age [90] that's the way it has to be)." This was followed by lines, dots and dashes along with her correction: "I bathe every day!!!"

After the birth of Frieda's daughter, there was no more Frieda for a while, but later on, she did come by, this time to the nursing home. These were the visits of a friend to a friend, not a client. "We get by with a little help from our friends," Frieda, Judy, and many other people of the "helping professions" helped me get by. Forgive the tirade, but why is it that our "advanced" societies place such little value on such a valuable resource: our old people? Both Frieda and Judy remain highly intelligent, resourceful, pragmatic, and affectionate people, and they took care of my mom lovingly, despite her contrariness, occasional insults, and bad-faith innuendos. Throughout those years, I marveled at how professional and sweet they were, and they deserved to be recognized with more than just an occasional gesture of gratitude. As women, they saw the value in my mom, in spite of it all. Yes, my mom was hard to bear, but there was always a liveliness, mischief, and sense of the absurd in everything she did. The problem was that you had to look for it, and Frieda and Judy were observant, alert, and attentive to her. Maybe for these women, my mom was something of a reflection of what they might or might not become.

Indeed, don't we all think about ending up in nursing homes? And isn't there always someone who says, "Not my mother; we'll never send her to one of those places"? I used to think this, and my brother affirmed it, but that's just where she spent the last three years of her life.

Chapter Twelve

The South Hampton Death House

From the Brattleboro Retreat to the Glencliff Sanatorium, and now to the final three years of life in Missouri in a nursing home, called South Hampton Place, another "place" of confinement, the last one.

It was her new residence, another institution, a place you go to when you're not well, but not a hospital—this is where you go and you never come back. I recently looked at South Hampton Place's web page and was stunned to learn that the average stay is three months, because what happens to the residents is that—surprise, surprise—they die. Why was I stunned? I suppose what gave me pause is that my mom, at her ripe age of ninety-three, outlasted most of the residents by a lot. But it wasn't like Glencliff or Brattleboro, because from this one she would not come back to the world of the living.

Reading the multi-page log book provided by Home Instead which I kept throughout those final years jotting down impressions, relating anecdotes that would appear in a book I'm writing about my mom, I see Mercedes' final years as a struggle to stay alive, a struggle that was becoming more and more difficult to wage; at times I sensed she had given up on it. As those who deal with loved ones with dementia know too well, that struggle is a precarious one, because with senility comes a loss of a sense of self. Indeed that's what was happening to Mercedes; her confusion was intensifying to the point that it was not clear if she herself knew what was happening to her mind and body. All she knew for sure was that she was getting old. Yes, she was now resigned it seems to accept that death was not far away.

The move from her apartment to this "Place" was unbearable. This time I'm sure of it. All her other life moves may have been difficult and precarious, but this last one was the result of a necessarily cruel act done to her by her younger son—so draconian, she could barely believe it was true. She must have told herself it was not.

As both Frieda and Judy were telling me, often in the gentlest terms, Mercedes, "God bless her," was becoming incapable of taking care of herself, and she needed permanent care. At times she left her front door unlocked or even open for God knows how long. Evidence of her incontinence was showing up in the apartment—of this I was all too aware. At one point I arrived at her place and found a portrait of her on the floor with the protective glass broken. It was a large and heavy painting with a garish frame, about three by four feet: Doña Mercedes in a black gown with a decorative Spanish fan in her hand and a *peineta* in her hair, one of those nineteenth-century combs worn by women of a certain importance to show off their hair. It was a cliché of the aristocratic Spanish woman (a bad imitation of Goya). I hated it, not like the other portrait of my mom—happy, smiling a little more genuinely than Mona Lisa, elegant but not pretentious. That one was safely in my house; later I took it to her room in the nursing home, and today it hangs in my study and it served to keep me from giving up on this book.

I asked her how the portrait, the pretentious one, landed on the floor, and she told me she had no idea. She didn't even seem surprised or bothered by it. What was going on in my mom's apartment when I wasn't there, or what was going on in her head, I will never know. The uncertainty was leading me to nursing homes. And when the time came, off we went to South Hampton Place with the pretense that she was going back to that "nice hotel" she had visited; she would stay here for a bit longer, for another visit and then she would go back to her apartment—I lied. I believe it was early in the evening. She and I were led by the nursing staff to a double room. Her roommate, a lady from Missouri, was nice enough until she heard us speaking Spanish. I looked at Mercedes and said something like, *"Te vas a quedar aquí esta noche"* (You're going to stay here tonight). She was confused for sure, but then again, she was always confused in these final years, so instead of sticking around to explain what was happening to her, I made sure an aid was around to settle her in, and I left. I felt my level of cruelty had overtaken me and that I would never be normal again.

But my mom was a survivor. She dealt with all the difficulties in her life by pretending they weren't true, as if all life is made of possibilities, circumstances, events, joys, sorrows, accidents, suicides, and other deaths that may or may not have happened. If they're life threatening, just ignore them because surely they will go away.

She eventually got used to her new dwelling. She had no choice. And then some good luck: a single room became available—no doubt someone died—so with the help of the staff, I moved her into the last of her bedrooms. It was a room with a five-star view of the parking lot; not exactly the Alicante seaside, but at least there were glimpses of sun. The first few months at the nursing home in her single room were filled with joys, sorrows, and extreme unpleasantness, a euphemism for hell. I'll be more blunt. My mom was at once constipated and incontinent and that condition seemed like it lasted an eternity.

From the last months in her apartment to the end—the most unbearable reality for me–it must have been pretty horrid for her too—was dealing with her shit. And I don't use that word figuratively. I apologize to anyone reading this who might be offended, but shit was a major part of her life; and it could happen to any of us. Desperately seeking a remedy to her urge to defecate without success, she would reach behind her and grope within the deepest reaches of her bowels or as far as she could and yank out a brown substance that would have made the least squeamish of us cringe. And when it comes to shit, I'm among the most squeamish. Why, I asked myself, was I not bothered by changing my two children's diapers countless times years ago? Yet doing the same for my mom was such an abysmal chore. And why do I find it easy to "curb"—how's that for a euphemism?—the dogs in my care? I'm not sure of the answer to that. Some of it has to do with being a man unaccustomed to taking care of other people's bodies. It could also be the fact that she was my mother, the one who called me Miguelito, the one who was pleased with my accomplishments, no matter how insignificant, and the one who laughed with me. None of that had anything to do with shit.

The protagonist of Rick Moody's famous 1997 novel, *Purple America*, seems to have a different view of this. Here is what the author says about taking care of his mom:

Whosoever knows the complexities of his own mother's body shall never die, ... [he] who has wiped stalactites of drool from his mother's mouth, ...

[wiped her ass] where a sweet infantile shit sometimes collects ... *he shall never die*" [emphasis his].

And the tone and content continue like this for several pages, all one paragraph ending the way he began, by saying that people like him will never drop dead.

My reaction when I read this was: Yeah right! And I wanted to respond to him: Nice rhetoric, Mr. Moody, but unlike you and your protagonist, I will surely not be spared death for having taken care of my mother's body. I've done most of the things you say—I have taken her into my arms and led her to her "baptismal" font, meaning the torture chamber of the bathroom where I guided her forcefully into the shower stall as she screamed, I have wiped the "stalactites" of drool from her face, and I've dipped a wet towel in water to wipe the grains of rice from the paella she had eaten, and more. I've taken her by her arm to help her upstairs or down a slight incline, swearing at her the whole way, I've tried (unsuccessfully) to wrap that damn hearing aid around her ears, I've cursed at her for yelling at me as I awkwardly trimmed her fingernails and (God forbid) her toenails with scissors meant for other things or nail cutters that she thought were torture instruments, I've shoveled unappetizing death house food—like Jell-O and creamed corn from a can—into her rejecting mouth, I've checked and found little turds and big turds in her bed-sheets, and I've lifted her stick figure body up to wipe her ass. And the times, many of them, I wiped my mother's butt, I did so with disgust, not only disgust, but anger and self-pity. I can see it in the log book, the one that turned into a book of notes for this very book. Taking care of my mother's shit, I say on various occasions, was the worst part of taking care of my mother.

So now someone tells me that for having done all this I'm not going to die? Surely Moody's protagonist was more gentle, and deserves a good pat on the back—but redemption, as in eternal life? If we are ever redeemed, it will certainly be for something else. I, like you, Mr. Moody, am going to die, and my hope is that I do so well before either of my two children has to wipe shit off my ass. Indeed, I've told them: once I start drooling, I give them permission to shoot me, because I'm way too much of a coward to do it myself.

But of course that's part of all this, not the whole story. There were lots of good moments in those years in South Hampton—death house notwithstanding—and several healthcare workers who treated my mom with much sympathy and tenderness. One in particular, Isabel, was a Spanish-speaker who had come to the U.S. from Mexico without proper papers. (For this reason I don't use her real name.) She and my mom hit it off immediately; she was the only aid at the Place that could carry on a conversation with Mercedes. Dementia plays all kinds of linguistic tricks on its victims: in the last two years of her life, my mom had forgotten virtually all of her English. So Isabel was a godsend. Most of the English-speaking care workers–in Columbia Missouri at that time, that meant just about all of them–seemed standoffish to my mom because they thought she couldn't speak English. In any case, as with most nursing homes, if the family does not insist that their loved one be given proper care, it just won't happen. Healthcare workers dealing with the elderly are among the lowest-paid professionals in the country. And some of them do their work with such tenderness and care that it should put us all to shame.

At times I descended into feeling sorry for myself, but at other times—I'd like to think it was most of the time—I treated my mom with respect and love, coaxing, cajoling, conversing, however incoherently, and best of all, laughing with her. And when she was in a good mood, that smile—mischievous, happy to see me—put adrenaline in my spirit. After all, I was her life, and I'm certain she was grateful. So instead of groveling in self-pity, I should keep in my memory all those times that I brought my mom home with me, where she ate, watched television, and read her *People* magazine and *TV Guide*. Several times I drove her back to South Hampton after both of us had drunk a few glasses of wine. If we had been stopped by Missouri's finest, we would probably both have ended up in another "fine hotel," one with iron bars instead of a door. But fortunately, to anyone in a squad car, the sight of an aging man driving with his ancient mother was surely not anything to cause suspicion. When we arrived at South Hampton, I imagine the nurse on duty noticed our peculiar behavior. How could anyone miss it? My mom would break into a chorus of the Marseillaise, of all the national hymns she could have sung:

Allons enfants de la Patrie,
Le jour de gloire est arrivé !
Contre nous de la tyrannie,

Aux armes, citoyens,
Formez vos bataillons,
Marchons, marchons!

And this time, unlike when she bellowed out the theme from *Dr. Zhivago* on a train in the middle of the Illinois steppes, I joined her in her operatic performance. I'm positive I messed up the words. She, on the other hand, surely got them right. As they say, a good time was had by the both of us, and even more so considering this woman was not too far from death.

Truth be told, in those days, taking care of my mom when I brought her to my house in Missouri was at times not only undemanding (not counting the shit), these were instances of real enjoyment. My mom surprised me at what she was able to do and what she was able to remember. She remembered my house; she had been there many times, and I'm not exactly proud of the fact that when she got there she did what she was used to doing for much of her life: she picked up the broom and started sweeping. Yes, I'm a male of Spanish descent, which means, among other things, that I was not required to clean, cook, or wash laundry as a child. Cleaning and laundry have always been a chore, but cooking is something I did take up. However, it was nothing my mom taught me. When her little Miguelito brought a cup of instant coffee to her bedroom on an occasional morning, she laughed with glee, knowing that it would never be my station in life to do the cooking. Numerous times Mercedes would sweep the front porch of my house, and my dear neighbor Susan, a woman who had been to Europe, told me, "Ah yes, those sweeping strokes—the sound of the Old World." Today I find it astounding that Mercedes found her way to a bedroom. Dementia may have taken its toll, but not when it comes to sweeping.

Mercifully, these were good times—except for when they weren't. Many hours of Mercedes' final two years were spent in bed doing absolutely nothing. The only thing that made her happy I think was when I walked into her room, and she recognized me. At times she thought I was her husband

Paco, but usually she recognized me as her son. Many times she exclaimed when I arrived, "¿*Tú quién eres, Miguel?*" (Who are you, Miguel?) Jorge and I are your only sons, I answered hoping she might remember one of us or both of us. But her question was a remarkably clever contradiction, typical of her speech and thinking, because I'm convinced she new exactly what she was asking. She was asking who I was in every sense, as in "Who the hell is this guy who just walked in here? Where does he come from? Why is he here? Why does he exist?" She blurted this out with a smile; those smiles were what I was living for at that time.

But what Mercedes was living for was something else. I sensed the intensification of her creeping uncertainty about her own aliveness. The good people in hospice had a term for it: "failure to thrive." It was a medical category, and it allowed her to have special benefits, like a hospice nurse to look after her and to talk to me about these final moments. Acknowledging failure to thrive made everything much easier. Everything, that is, except the constipation and the bathing.

South Hampton had a rule of two showers a week for their residents. Thank God those showers were not my responsibility, but Lord help those poor souls in charge of wheeling my mom down the hall to the shower room to bathe her. For my mom it was pure dread—horrific, agonizing, something that would lead to certain, slow and painful death. She was convinced she was the victim of abuse, and she let everyone around her know it. Something like the gas houses at the extermination camps. The yells and pleas for help were the noises of that poor woman in Picasso's *Guernica* looking up at the sky as the bombs fell. I was reminded of the way she said "Obuuuuuses" (shell explosions) when she remembered the Civil War. What she did yell was "Poliiiice!" (one of the few English words she still remembered), *and "¡Que me mueroooo!"* (I'm gonna die), and "*¡Que me maaaatan!"* (They're gonna kill me), and *"Mieeerda!"* (Shit), and lots of other expletives barely intelligible among the screams. Sometimes I waited in her room as they took her away, trying not to hear the cries of bloody murder. But astoundingly, when she got back to the room she was fine, better than fine—she felt more comfortable than she had felt in days. Invariably after those torture sessions, she slept, and she slept well. Indeed, most of those years at South Hampton she spent sleeping. Numerous times when I got to her room she was asleep, and a couple of hours later she was still sleeping, so after the advice I had gotten from hospice, I let her sleep, and after I left I had things to do.

I'd like to think she knew I had things to do: a job, a house, colleagues, friends. So even though she did not acknowledge both my entrance and my departure, she gave me her approval. That's what I like to think. Maybe it was her way of thanking me for giving her chocolates. What's wrong with that? Not only did I allow her to eat chocolates, I brought them to her, and she loved them. It was the only thing she was eating. Her weight got down to seventy-one pounds, but I no longer worried about it, or tried not to. I was waiting for her to die. I say it clearly in the log book several times. And I have said this to many people who have asked me about my mother's final years of life: "She was dead before she was dead." But I did not say, "I wish she would die soon." At least I didn't say this out loud.

And then she died. It was a few days after Christmas, 2008. On December 27, I went to San Francisco to visit with my son and his soon to be spouse, Hillary. I attended the Modern Language Association annual convention for that year. I got a call from South Hampton; they said my mom had a bad cold, that she was coughing a lot. I suspected the end was close, so why didn't I just return to Columbia immediately? I'll never know. I surmised, as I had done so many times before, that my mom would get over this; she always did. That she had a cold? That she was coughing? Could be true and not happening. My son and I went to his favorite place in the San Francisco area: Muir Woods. I could not get my mind off Mercedes. The next day a South Hampton nurse called to tell me she had died, so I went back to Columbia feeling awful and guilty, with my son following on one of the next flights. To this day I have not forgiven myself for not rushing back to Columbia.

She had two death services, twice so that the proper people could attend her funeral(s). The first time was in Columbia, Missouri, a town she called home, maybe even more of a home to her than Hellín. By now Hellín wasn't even a memory to her. I strongly suspect she did not remember her home town, but I'll never know. She was far away. Was she ever in that town in La Mancha? Could be true. She died in Columbia so we could all honor her and remember her life. Many people came to bid goodbye; as I said earlier, more than I imagined would come. We remembered her publicly with a DVD of one of her favorite singers playing in the background. Yes, none other than

Josephine Baker, a Harlem Renaissance singer living in Paris in the thirties, crooning about the bananas that covered her body—not all of it. My mom and dad saw her perform in Madrid.

J'ai deux amours, Mon pays et Paris.

(I have two loves, My country and Paris.

For Mercedes, Josephine Baker could very well have sung, " I have two loves, my country and Madrid." I learned of Mercedes' love for Josephine Baker's music when she was in her nineties, a lesson to all of us: we need to ask our aging moms and dads about their lives before it's too late.

The second funeral was in her other home town, Hanover, New Hampshire, about a year later. My brother George came with his family. A fine tribute to Mercedes with some of my friends, like Dennis, my best friend since second grade, and hers (the few still alive) paying respects. She would have loved that second funeral had she been there—but of course she was, and I don't mean in the form of cremated ashes. She was there in the forests surrounding the cemetery, looking at us all and laughing like Medusa. She heard my brother say a few words, and in spite of all those not-so-pleasant memories, she was happy that we were all together as a family. That's what death provides: togetherness and obliteration of the bad things.

I have fond memories of my brother at my mom's second funeral. George, the one named for that famous anti-imperialist George, the little boy who made that trip bridging two continents, the one who sadly had become estranged from Mercedes in her late years, but he came back to see her, and I'm sure she knew it. That George was with us all looking at my mom's ashes in an urn lying next to Paco in the Pine Knolls Cemetery in Hanover. During that second funeral I was remembering the time I spent with him painting my mother's deck attached to the house in West Lebanon. Mercedes had as much fun as we did. It took us a week or so, but we got it done. Although we did it wrong. Of course a varnish or wood protection would have been far better, as well as a professional opinion from someone, anyone in the Upper Valley of the Connecticut River. Less than a few months later, the paint began to fade and peel. But who cared? At the time, Grandma Mercedes was in her element, charmed, overjoyed that her boys and our friend Dennis were fussing over her, talking about what was best for her, correcting her bad habits (or what we thought were her bad habits).

The Upper Valley is not breathtakingly beautiful like, for example, Muir Woods, or Big Sur—a scenic wonder that Paco and Mercedes saw when they visited George in the sixties—or even the ravishing rocky coastline south of Biarritz on the border of France and Spain where my mom spent several years as a young girl. The beauty of the Upper Valley is subtle: gently rolling evergreen-wooded forests, a greenery so green that its contrast with La Mancha is palpable, so much so that her second-born son couldn't wait to get back after months in Spain when he was a boy. Mercedes loved the Upper Valley, even though she was never one to extoll natural beauty in excess. But everyone around her knew she enjoyed her surroundings. That's where she is now—Pine Knolls Cemetery in Hanover, both in the trees and in her casket, nagging at Paco to move over: *"Por Dios, Paco, que no me dejas ni respirar."* (For God's sake, Paco, you don't even let me breathe). The Connecticut River, in all its splendor, is about three hundred meters away from the burial ground, although you can't see it from where they lie. But George and I could see it when we went for a jog together, taking a break from painting Mercedes' deck, so close to her final resting place.

Nostalgia is, more often than not, a lie. But that memory of Jorge and Miguel running through the paths of the cemetery, through the woods, over a trail that runs within a stone's throw of the Connecticut, the river that shaped our lives—and hers—is a memory that I own, and I don't care if it's a lie. A lie only in the interpretation, but this one *is* true and *did* happen. After we finished the job on my mom's deck and George went home, I visited Mercedes often, and I always made a point to go for a jog to the cemetery where Paco was buried and on along to the river trail, remembering many things as I ran: my brother, my father, my mother. One day, as I was running along the cemetery paths, I saw the following inscription on the gravestone of someone buried near my dad's grave:

And when he shall die,
Take him and cut him out in little stars,
And he will make the face of heaven so fine
That all the world will be in love with night
And pay no worship to the garish sun.

The attribution was to Shakespeare, but I didn't realize it was from *Romeo and Juliet* until Google told me so. Of course, a heartfelt engraving for a loved one. And for my mom it would have been fitting as well, if I had thought of it. That is, as long as we included the words that precede these soothing lines:

"Give me my Romeo."

That's how I want to remember Mercedes—no matter if I've invented it, no matter that her love for Paco may not have been as reciprocal as it should have been, no matter if all this is true and didn't happen, no matter what a bitch she could be when she set her mind to it, no matter all the pitfalls of a mother's unconditional love for her two ungrateful sons, no matter how beautifully ridiculous she sounded when she paid tribute to her desires by saying "holy palmers' keeess," no matter how miserable she made my dad in his moments of despair; none of that matters. Yes, that's how I want to remember her as she talks to me from her grave—I can hear it as I write: *"Ahora hablaré de mí. Miguel, ayúdame"* (Now I'll speak about myself, Miguel, help me).

Epilogue

A Speck in the Horizon

I found this little piece among all the stuff related to Mercedes I had been gathering in boxes for I don't know how many years. Someone wrote it—I don't know who—probably around the time I moved her into the nursing home, judging from the other things I found in that box, all keepsakes of Mercedes' life in Missouri. It was probably me trying to say goodbye to my mother Mercedes and wishing her a happy journey. Like my story of my mother's life, it could be true and not have happened:

> She was ninety-six; I was sixty-nine. She weighed her age in pounds; I weighed considerably more. It was all I could do to keep her from disappearing from the map. I'd make "gambas al ajillo" (shrimp in olive oil and garlic), "pisto manchego" (tomato, zucchini, peppers, and onions), "patatas bravas" (potatoes in spicy tomato sauce), freshly butchered roasted chicken, and rice, always lots of rice. She ate everything I put in front of her, but she never exceeded her weight in years. With every birthday she got a little heftier, but not enough to catch up with the number of years since her birth. I resigned myself to the fact that I couldn't do anything about it: that's the way it was going to be. I would keep cooking, eating, and getting rounder, and she would keep eating and not getting round enough.
>
> As always, I waved to her from the beach. That was our pattern: in the mornings I would go down to the shore and

take the sun before going to the market, while she sat on the balcony looking at me, making sure I didn't go too far. Every day I would wave to her before I sat down on the sand.

But one day it all turned wild. For some reason she kept waving and pointing to the sky. I didn't make anything of it until I noticed one of those sinister gusts of wind getting up from its slumber to show the world how angry it was.

Without warning, the day had gone from sunny and pleasant to treacherous, one of those days when everything looks splendid until you hear the awnings flapping and the windows rattling. The wind was hitting the water hard; it seemed to blow from the north as the waves grew from ripples to twice, three, four times their normal size. The palm trees were bending away from the shoreline toward the mountains as if they wanted to run for cover, but they were stuck.

She looked terrified as she hung on to the balcony and gestured, trying to get me to come back. The wind didn't want to subside; it made her fingers lose grip of the grating. It looked like she was screaming as that wind took her southwestward along the balcony, going in the opposite direction from me. I stood up and called out, telling her to stay calm, that I would be there as soon as I could. But the same wind that freed her from the railing knocked me back down to the sand. As I got up, slowly she rose toward the clouds like she was on a kite some ten feet up from the balcony, then down about half that distance, and then up again even higher.

All I could do was watch. I wanted to tell her to hang on, but the powerful breeze caught my words. No matter how much or how loud I yelled, she couldn't hear; no one could hear anything except the sound of blowing. It was as if that wind were ordering me to shut my mouth and stay put.

I looked up. To my amazement, she didn't look scared anymore; as she kept gliding upward, she even seemed to smile. I could barely see her now; the distance between us was growing with every new gust. She soared up, then straight along the shoreline, then down, then up again. At one point she was almost as high as the building we were living in. I saw her flapping her spindly arms like a gull. She glided for several seconds, then flapped her arms again. I thought I saw her gesturing to me from up above, but I couldn't figure out what she was trying to tell me. Then she put her arms to her side and soared down about twenty feet to get close enough so I could hear her.

"*Adiós, Miguel, adiós, adiós. Me voy.*" One of her bony hands moved from her lips toward me. Then with a determination she had been storing up from the day she cried out for her mother as she lay dying, from the day she first saw Asis, from the day her father's death sentence was reduced to eight years in prison, from the day the shell exploded a few feet from where she lived, from the day she got on the boat that would take her to a new continent, from the day she was unable to nurse her firstborn son, from the day they took her second son away from her, from the day they put her in an asylum, from the day they made her lie in ice packs, from the day she recited Shakespeare in public, from the moment her husband threw himself into the gorge, from the day she left the house where she had cooked and cleaned for over three decades, from her first day of solitude, from the moment she left her home again to be close to her second-born son, from the day she asked, "Who are you, Miguel?"—from that day on, she had the ninety-six pounds it took to start flapping her arms to get up off the balcony and finally go to where she wanted to go.

I watched as she soared up over and under the clouds until she started fading away. She got smaller and smaller—a dot in the horizon that I could barely distinguish. The speck was trying to tell me something. I thought I heard words like, "*Adiós, Miguel. Que me voy para estar con Paco—para hacerle la vida imposible.*" (Goodbye, Michael. I'm off to be with Paco—to make his life impossible.)

Mercedes, on her way to work at the Gallery in the Hopkins Center
Dartmouth College; circa 1975

Sebastion, (not his real name)
Mercedes' first boyfriend
circa 1984

Mercedes throwing frisbee, West
Lebanon, New Hampshire; circa 1990

Mercedes
West Lebanon, New Hampshire; circa 1988

Mercedes with her brother Artemio, Amaya (Artemio's daughter), and Marti (Amaya's son)
Madrid; circa 1990

Michael (the author), my aunt Maruja, my aunt Marina
Albacete, Spain; circa 1993

Mercedes and her granddaughter, Maura (Molly)
Alicante; circa 1992. Photo by Kim Schäfermeyer

Mercedes arguing with her grandson, Francisco (Cisco)
Alicante; circa 1995

Mercedes on Muchavista Beach
Alicante, 2000

Mercedes, holding photos of her second boyfriend, Paulino (not his real name)
Columbia, Missouri; circa 2002

Mercedes and Michael reciting poetry
Artisan Cafe; Columbia, Missouri
2002

Mercedes with "Miguel el Superior"
Columbia, Missouri; circa 2003

Mercedes with Michael
Columbia, Missouri, circa 2004. Photo by Maura Ugarte

Mercedes and Miguel (Michael)
Madrid; circa 2005

Francisco (Cisco) and Mercedes
Madrid; circa 2005

Francisco (Cisco) and Mercedes
Madrid; circa 2005

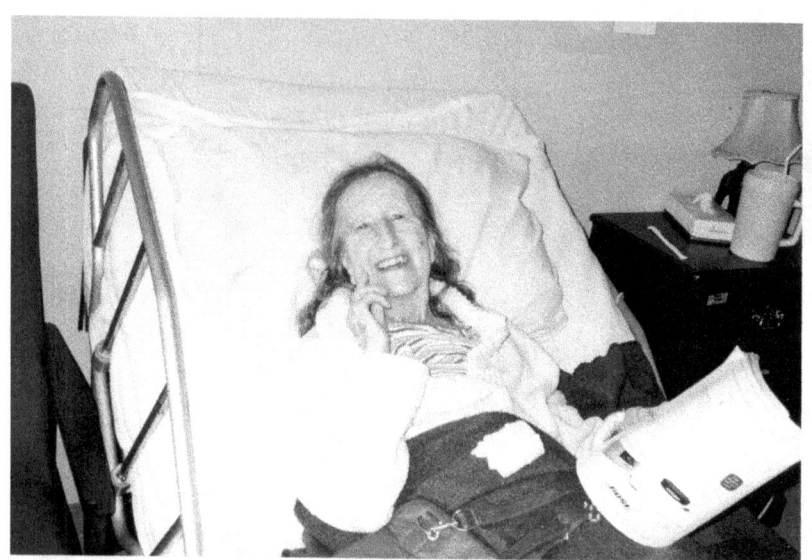

Mercedes. South Hampton Place
Columbia, Missouri; 2007

Mercedes. South Hampton Place
Columbia, Missouri; 2007

Mercedes Precioso Ugarte Family Tree

To the reader:
Surnames in the Hispanic World are used in the following way:
Given Name(s) followed by father's surname followed by mother's surname. As in Mercedes (given name) Precioso (her father's surname) Ugarte (her mother's surname).
Michael (Miguel) (given name) Ugarte (my dad's surname) Precioso (my mom's surname).
I have diagrammed this as follows:

The Preciosos

José Precioso Roche (1865-1903) married to Teófila García Silvestre had several children: **Artemio**, Octavio, Encarnación and others

Artemio Precioso García (son of José) (1891-1945) married to Marina Ugarte Cristóbal (1889-1918) had three children: **Mercedes** (1913-2008), Marina, Artemio

Artemio Precioso García married second marriage to Amelia Precioso de la Fuente circa 1920 had three children: Maruja, Soledad, Amelia

The Ugartes

Eliano Ugarte Uhagón (1841-?) married Elizabeth Schultz: had several children:
Francisco Javier Ugarte Schultz (son of Eliano) (1869-1949) married Micaela Cristóbal Ibarzábal had eight children: Javier, Juan José, **Francisco (Asis, Paco)** (1910-1969), Marina (my mom's mom), Alfonso, Joaquín, Fernando, Ana María

Francisco Ugarte Cristóbal (1910-1969) married Mercedes Precioso Ugarte (1913-2008) had two children: George (Jorge) (1943-2017), Michael (Miguel) (b. 1949)

Related reading

There are countless books on the Spanish Civil War. Helen Graham's *The Spanish Civil War: A Very Short Introduction* (Oxford University Press, 2005) is an excellent synopsis and explanation of the main issues and events.

Paul Preston is among the many British historians who has written about the Spanish Civil War. His *Last Days of the Spanish Republic* (Harper Collins, 2016) discusses Mercedes' brother Artemio Precioso Ugarte's military role in the final months before Franco's victory.

Hotel Florida: Truth, Love, and Death in the Spanish Civil War, a lively documentary novel about Ernest Hemingway and Martha Gellhorn by Amanda Vail (Bloomsbury, 2014) is worth reading, although a bit too melodramatic for my tastes. A personal note of caution to readers: beware of facile analyses and reenactments of the Spanish Civil War. It's always more complicated than described. Even George Orwell's famous *Homage to Catalonia* (Harvill Secken, 1938, first ed.) has to be taken in stride. He wrote this classic before the war's end.

In addition to stories and novels, Martha Gellhorn, from St. Louis, MO, wrote stirring journalistic pieces about what she saw in Spain and in the rest of Europe during the turbulent thirties and forties, *Face of War* (Virago, 1985).

There is an unjustly overlooked literary memoir by Josephine Herbst (Harper Collins, 1960) about Spanish and world politics of the war years, an excellent and thoughtful assessment about a kind of writing that sacrifices human ambiguity to politics.

A recent edition of the novel I reference at the beginning of Chapter Four, *Celia en la revolución* (Celia in the Revolution, Renacimiento, 2016) has an informative and stirring introduction by the well-known literary critic, Andrés Trapiello. Some might categorize it as a "young adult" novel which is the genre the author, Elena Fortún, is most known for. Yet this novel contains many adult themes, such as war time violence, death, and suffering. As far as I know it has not been translated into English.

I have written a biographical piece about my uncle, "Artemio Precioso Ugarte (1917-2007): An Avuncular Environmental Activist in Spain," for *Hispanic Issues: Environmental Cultural Studies*: https://cla.umn.edu/sites/cla.umn.edu/files/hiol_24_14_ugarte.pdf

If you read Spanish, here is a biography of my uncle (Artemio Jr.) by an environmental activist, Jordi Bigues, *Artemio Precioso Ugarte (1917-2007): la lealtad y el entusiasmo* (Instituto de Estudios Albacetenses, 2018).

Also, if you read Spanish, Francisco Linares' edition of Artemio Precioso García's (Artemio Sr.) book about his exile in France in the 1920s, *Españoles en el destierro* (Instituto de Estudios Albacetenses, 2016) has an extensive introduction about my grandfather's life.

Linares's complete biography of my grandfather, Artemio Precioso García has been released: *Apuntes biográficos sobre el escritor y editor Artemio Precioso García (1891- 1945)*, Instituto de Estudios Albacetenses, 2021.

Mercedes' father, Artemio Precioso García, has been the subject of historical and literary discussion. Again for Spanish readers, Manuel Arnaldos edited a volume of my grandfather's selected fiction, *Artemio Precioso y la novella corta* (Colección Arkanos, 1997).

In addition *Kiosk Literature of Silver Age Spain: Modernity and Mass Culture* edited by Jeffrey Zamostny and Susan Larson (Intellect 2017) is an excellent collection of essays about popular literature in Spain dealing with magazines, novels, novellas, cartoons, and other graphic material widely sold in newsstands (*kioscos*) in the twenties and thirties when my grandfather was a well-known writer and editor.

Take note that Zamostny has translated into English one of Elena Fortún's major writings, a semi-autobiographical novel, *Hidden Path* (Swan Isle Press, 2021). Fortún is the author of the *Celia* young adult novels including *Celia in the Revolution*).

On a similar subject, Maite Zubiaurre's *Cultures of the Erotic in Spain. 1898-1939* (Vanderbilt Univ. Press, 2012) is a lively analysis published by a university press, but don't let that fool you. Some might call it ex-rated. The photos capture readers' eyes in all sorts of ways. It's great reading too. Zubiaurre talks about my grandfather as a figure who was and remains a major player in the public discussion and dissemination of "the erotic" in Spain in the 1920s and 30s.

The issue of "historical memory" of the Spanish Civil War remains a hot topic in today's Spain. Since the death of Franco, many Spaniards have searched archives and asked eyewitnesses about their loved ones' participation in the War. Sebastiaan Faber's, *Memory Battles of the Spanish Civil War* (Vanderbilt Univ. Press, 2017) is an excellent discussion and analysis of controversies that have arisen as a result of new readings and citizens' investigations of Spanish history. Faber's treatment makes a point of going beyond academic discussions of the issue. He engages his readers with his questions about the different ways a given group might interpret events in their history. If you read Spanish I have written an extensive review of this work for an on-line Spanish journal, *FronteraD* (https://www.fronterad.com/una-lectura-personal-de-un-ensayo-de-sabastiaan-faber-sobre-la-memoria-de-las-batallas-de-la-guerra-civil-espanola/).

In a more general vein David Rieff's *In Praise of Forgetting: Historical Memory and Its Ironies* (Yale Univ. Press, 2017) is a conceptual questioning of that oft-cited phrase, "Those who cannot remember their past are condemned to repeat it." Sometimes it's better to forget, he says. A more accessible version of his philosophical arguments is in an essay he wrote for the *The Guardian*, "The Cult of Memory: When History Does More Harm Than Good": https://www.theguardian.com/education/2016/mar/02/cult-of-memory-when-history-does-more-harm-than-good.

The artist Art Spiegelman's famous graphic novel *Maus* is about his personal attempt to come to terms with what happened to his family during the years before, during and after Hitler's "Final Solution." For many years that work has haunted me, and when my daughter reminded me of it when I told her I was writing about Mercedes, I went back to it.

It's no secret that writing about your mother presents problems of all kinds. *Mothers*, a special issue of *Granta: The Magazine of New Writing* (88, Winter 2004), has some touching and compelling essays and artistic pieces by authors remembering their mothers or commenting on the concept of motherhood.

In the same vein *Mothers [and] Sons: In their Own Words*, Mariana Cook (Chronicle Books, 1996) is a coffee-table book of photographic portraits of mothers with their sons. I gave Mercedes a copy of this book on Mother's Day 1996.

As many memoirists will point out—Mary Karr is one of the most prominent—the memoir is a special genre, it's non-fiction that seems at times like fiction, depending on the author's inclinations. I read many as I was writing about my mom. Maybe the memoir that hit me the hardest is Richard Ford's *Between Them: Remembering My Parents* (Harper Collins, 2017). Ford writes about his mom and dad as two separate entities. The first part is about his dad and the second is about his mom. He artfully fuses both of them.

www.ingramcontent.com/pod-product-compliance
Lightning Source LLC
Chambersburg PA
CBHW071114160426
43196CB00013B/2571